Australian

Baby names

+ memories

Daphne Attwood

For my wonderful Mom, with love

is an imprint of Publishing
Management Pty Ltd
(A.C.N. 059 642 045)
PO Box 529
Kiama NSW 2533 Australia
Telephone: (042) 331773

ISBN: 1-875666-08-7

Cartoons by
MARK ELDER

Printed by
McPherson's Printing Group
Maryborough, Victoria,
Australia

*Wholly designed and typeset in
Australia by*
Southern Media Services
PO Box 529 Kiama NSW 2533

Contents

My name is

. . . .

My parents are

. . . .

. . . .

I was born on

. . . .

at exactly . . . . . am/pm. . . . .

at . . . .

I was delivered by . . . .

. . . .

This is me just after I was born.

This is me just after I was born.
Holding me is . . . .

This is how I announced my arrival.

The newspaper advertisement used

more words:

Picking my name was fun. These

were the names my parents liked:

Boy	Girl
. . . .	. . . .
. . . .	. . . .
. . . .	. . . .

This is me at . . . . . months with . . . .

. . . . .

This is me at . . . . . month with . . . . .

. . . . .

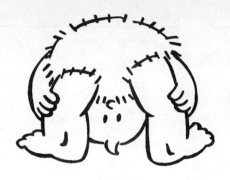

LOOK HOW I GREW

Age	Weight	Height
At birth		
1 Week		
2 Weeks		
3 Weeks		
4 Weeks		
1 Month		
2 Months		
3 Months		
6 Months		
1 Year		

This is me at . . . . . months with . . . .

. . . .

This is me at . . . . . months with . . . .

. . . .

MY VERY FIRST ...

☆ *WORD was* ....

and was spoken on ....

☆ *STEP was taken on* ....

☆ *TOOTH appeared on* ....

☆ *SHOES were size* ....

☆ *SOLID FOOD was*.............

....

which I ate on ....

☆ *NIGHT WITHOUT WAKING*

my parents even once was

....

This is me at . . . . . months with . . . . .

. . . .

This is me at . . . . . . month with . . . . .

. . . .

MY FAVOURITE ...

Foods are

. . . .

Toys are

. . . .

Activities are

1 Month. . . . .

2 Months. . . . .

3 Months. . . . .

6 Months. . . . .

9 Months. . . . .

12 Months. . . . .

. . . .

This is me at . . . . . months with . . . .

. . . . .

This is me at . . . . . month with . . . . .

. . . . .

MY FIRST CHRISTMAS

Look at me on Christmas Day

with . . . .

. . . . .

. . . . .

. . . . .

Santa brought me these exciting gifts

. . . . .

. . . . .

. . . . .

MY FIRST BIRTHDAY

I am ONE YEAR OLD today!

Look at me with . . . .
. . . .
. . . .
. . . .

I had a great party at which we . . . .
. . . .
. . . .
. . . .
. . . .

Tips on selecting your baby's name

AFTER LIFE itself, the name you give your baby is the first - and most personal - gift you bestow on your infant. Choosing that very special name is a joyful experience, one which every parent agonises over for many hours at an end.

But it is also a task you should approach with some care, because the name you decide on today is the name your child will (hopefully) still be using 60 or 70 years in the future.

Here are some suggestions to guide you while deciding on a name for your baby.

Family names

Sometimes, especially with a first child, you have little choice, because family tradition lays down what you should name your son or daughter. But remember, you can always add another name of your own choosing, either as a first or a second name.

One couple I know decided to name their baby boy after his paternal grandfather, David Andrew, but changed it very slightly to David Andrè, keeping the same initials and sound, but giving the baby a unique combination.

Another way to please the family while being different is to reverse the family names: Catherine Eveline could become Eveline Catherine.

Another way to satisfy family tradition while still being different, is to vary the spelling: Tiffany, Lucy and Simon still sound the same even when spelled Tyffany, Luci and Syman.

Parents' names

Often people combine the names of mother and father when choosing one for their child. My friends Peter and Dorothea, for instance, named their daughter Perthea.

Or, if you want to keep the parental link without being too obvious, consider translating a parental name into another language: John's son could become Sean, Ian or Juan (Irish, Scottish or Spanish, respectively).

Also growing in popularity is to give the baby the mother's maiden name as one (usually the second) name: Sandra McLennan and Russell Jones named their son William McLennan Jones. Or you can link the mother's maiden name by hyphen to the father's surname, giving your baby a hyphenated surname such as Digby-Smythe.

Nicknames

Babies are cute and cuddly, but choosing a name that reflects that cuteness almost certainly will prove an embarrassment for the child as a teenager and later in life. If you like the names Suzy, Harry or Teddy, for instance, it is easy enough to ensure you can use it as a nickname by registering the more serious names Suzanne, Harold or Edward on the birth certificate. That gives your son or daughter a choice when he or she gets older.

On the other hand, there's every chance that Rebecca will be Becky and Richard will be Dick to their friends, so if you happen to hate those nicknames, it's probably best to avoid the related names and look for something completely different.

Funny names

If you have a son named Jack, don't be tempted to call his sister Jill - chances are the two will pay a price for it later in the schoolyard, particularly if they are twins. Say the name aloud so that you know what it sounds like, paired with the family name. So if your family is called Good, naming your child William Bertram Good could well lead to him being teased as "Will B. Good".

Odd or long names

When Mr and Mrs James Williams decided to reflect the famed size of their native Texas in the name they bestowed on their daughter in 1984, they settled on R h o s h a n d i a t e l l y n e s h i a u n n e v e s h e n k Koyaanfsquatsiuty Williams. Three weeks later, however, they decided it was not impressive enough, so they officially expanded her first name to 1,019 letters and the middle name to 36 letters.

This won the family an entry in the *Guinness Book of Records*, but almost certainly also earned their child a lifetime of problems and embarrassment.

And while on the subject of odd names, imagine being the son or daughter of rock star Frank Zappa: the boy is called Dweezil and the girl Moon Unit!

Particularly in our computer age, make sure the names you choose are short enough to fit into those little blocks provided on official forms - choose too long a name and your child will be left dangling halfway through all future official correspondence.

There is increasing evidence that giving your child an unusual name may have negative repercussions in school, according to noted US psychologist Dr Herbert Harari, of San Diego State University. In his major study several groups of primary school teachers, when presented with compositions written by students with currently fashionable names like Michael, David, Karen and Lisa, awarded them one or more grades higher than students with unfashionable names like Elmer, Hubert and Bertha. Yet *all* the compositions had been judged by independent researchers to be of equal standard. Dr Harari believes society may be subconsciously prejudiced against certain names.

Number of names

A multitude of first names has always been a royal tradition (often used to cement all the alliances in place at the time), but very few blue-bloods come close to the great-great-grandson of King Carlos III of Spain. Don Alfonso de Borbon y Borbon, who died in 1934 at the age of 68, had 94 first names, several of which were lengthened by hyphenation.

But Britons John and Margaret Nelson of Chesterfield, Derbyshire, topped every royal record in December 1985 when they named their daughter Tracy - followed by 138 other first names!

In a multicultural country such as Australia, the number of names given to children vary greatly. The current fashion, according to researchers, is for two first-names, perhaps influenced by the American demand for a middle initial (which caused President Harry S. Truman to invent his middle initial, even though it stood for nothing, because he lacked a middle name!).

Always bear in mind that too many names can cause embarrassment at school or when completing forms that require you to list all your names. Ask yourself seriously: does our child really need more than two, or at most three, names?

Check the meaning

Bethany is a nice sounding name, but would you be happy to be branded forever as a "house of poverty"? Or "dim-sighted", which is exactly what Cecil indicates?

It's also a good idea to avoid names with negative associations: Kermit may mean "free" in Irish, but any Australian child with that name will always be linked on the playground with a frog. And after the success of the *Life. Be In It* series, would you really like your son to be associated with Norm? Likewise, any boy named

Adolf is likely to suffer throughout childhood, while Flora and margarine are just to closely linked to be kind.

Initials can spell disaster

Before you rush off to register your baby's name, jot down the initials. Felicity Alison Thomas may sound great to you, but chances are kids at school will quickly latch on to her initials and call her "Fat". Likewise, Veronica Davis could be in for a bumpy ride as teenagers experiment with sexually risque words and phrases.

Sound the name

Practise saying the names you like for your baby over and over again - you'll quickly reject quite a number of combinations because they just don't sound right together. And be sure to include your family name in the sounding process. Experts say a last name with one-syllable usually is best combined with a first name of two or more syllables: Elizabeth Kemp pleases the ear much more than Liz Kemp. Likewise, it is claimed a two-syllable surname sounds best when combined with a first name of three or four syllables: for instance, Elizabeth Taylor or Patricia Stephens.

If you're keen to make the names sound as though they really belong together, try alliteration, or names that have a similar initial sound: Patricia Priestly and Sylvester Stallone are good examples.

Is it a boy or a girl?

Unisex names are popular with many parents, although it is a good idea to use the spelling to indicate gender: for instance, Tony for a boy and Toni for a girl. But be careful, particularly with boys, not to bestow a name which is usually considered female: I know men named Francis, Beverly and Vivian who all admit they were teased unmercifully throughout their school careers and even today hide behind "Frank", "Bev" or "Viv".

Fashion

Enjoy fashion - but don't be a slave to it. That dictum also applies to choosing a name for your baby: what sounds trendy today could very quickly become outmoded, but unlike an unfashionable item of clothing, your son or daughter can't discard a name quite as quickly or easily. Names like Sunshine, Moon, and Peace, popular during the Age of Aquarius, are decidedly out of place today.

Finally ...

Ask yourself : would I like to have that name as my own? If you don't, think again. If you do, chances are it's the right choice.

Names
for
GIRLS

A

Abaigeal *(Irish)* Gail

Abbey *See* Abigail

Abigail *(Hebrew)* Source of joy

Abra *(Hebrew)* Mother of many

Acacia *(Greek)* Thorny

Acantha *(Greek)* Thorny

Achilla *(Greek) Feminine of* Achilles

Acton *(Old English)* Village with oak trees

Ada *(Old English)* Prosperous/joyous/noble

Adah *(Hebrew)* Tiara/crown

Adalia *(Old German)* Noble

Adamina *(Latin) Feminine of* Adam

Adan *(English)* Aidan

Adar *(Hebrew)* Fiery

Adara *(Greek)* Beauty

Adelaide *(Old German)* Noble

Adelheid *(German)* Noble

Adelicia *(Old English)* Alice

Adeline *See* Adelaide

Adina *(Australian Aboriginal)* Good

Aditi *(Hindi)* One who is free, unrestrained

Adolpha *(Old German)* She-wolf

Adonia *(Greek)* Beautiful

Adora-belle *(French)* Adored and beautiful

Adora *(Latin)* Glorious gift/glory/fame

Adoria *See* Adora

Adorlee *(French)* One who is adored

Adorna *(Latin)* Decorated with jewels

Adria *(Latin) See* Adriana

Adriana *(Latin)* Swarthy

Adrienne *(Latin)* Dark lady

Aerona *(Welsh)* Like a berry

Agata *(Irish, Italian)* Agatha

Agatha *(Greek)* Good

Agave *(Greek)* Noble/high ranking

Aggie *See* Agnes

Agnella *See* Agnes

Agnes *(Greek)* Pure

Agnese *(Italian)* Agnes

Agneta *(Swedish, Danish)* Agnes

Agrippina *(Latin)* Born feet first

Agueda *(Spanish)* Agatha

Ahuda *(Hebrew)* Praise

Aida *(Italian)* Ada

Aidan *(Irish)* Small fire

Aileen *(Irish)* Carrier of light. *Also Irish form of* Helen

Ailey *See* Aileen

Ailis *(Irish)* Alice

Ailsa *(Old German)* Cheerful girl

Aimée *(French)* Amy

Aindrea *(Irish)* Andrea

Aingeal *(Irish)* Angela

Ainsley *(Scottish)* Clearing in your own meadow

Airleas *(Irish)* A pledge

Aisha *(Swahili)* Life

Aislinn *(Irish Gaelic)* Dream/vision

Akuna *(Australian Aboriginal)* Follower

Alameda *(Spanish)* Poplar

Alana *(Celtic)* Fair

Alba *(Australian Aboriginal)* Wind

Albania *(Italian)* Albinia

Alberta *(Old English)* Noble

Albinia *(Latin)* White/blonde

Alcina *(Greek)*
Strong-willed

Alcyon *(Greek)* Peaceful

Alda *(Old German)* Wise
or wealthy old person

Aldora *(Old English)*
High-ranking/noble

Aleen *(English)* Aileen

Alejandra *(Spanish)*
Alexandra

Alene *See* Aileen

Aleria *(Latin)* Like an
eagle

Alesia *(Greek)* Helper

Alessandra *(Italian)*
Alexandra

Aleta *(Latin)* Like a bird

Aletea *(Spanish, Italian)*
Alethia

Alethea *(Greek)* Truthful

Aletta *See* Alethea

Alex *See* Alexandra

Alexandra *(Greek)*
Defender of mankind

Alexandrine *(French)*
Alexandra

Alexis *See* Alexandra

Aleza *(Hebrew)* Joyfull

Alfonsine *(Old German)*
Noble

Alfreda *(Old English)*
Wise counsellor/elf

Alice *(Greek)* Truth

Alicea *See* Alice

Alicia *(Italian, Spanish,
Swedish)* Alice

Alida *(Latin)* Winged

Alima *(Arabic)*
Dancer/musician

Alima *(Arabic)* One who
knows dancing/music

Alina *(Slavic)*
Bright/good looking

Alinga *(Australian
Aboriginal)* The sun

Alisa *(Italian)* Alice

Alison *(Irish)* Truthful

Alissa *See* Alice

Alithia *See* Alice

Alkira *(Australian
Aboriginal)* The sky

Allegra *(Italian)*

Cheerful/happy

Allene *See* Alanna

Allie *See* Alice

Allira *(Australian Aboriginal)* Quartz

Allison *(Irish)* Small

Allys *See* Alice

Alma *(Hebrew)* Young woman

Almira *(Arabic)* Exalted/Truth

Aloha *(Hawaiian)* Greetings/farewell

Aloysia *(Old German)* Fighter. *Feminine of* Moses

Alpha *(Greek)* First one

Alta *(Latin)* Lofty/elevated

Althea *(Greek)* Healer/Wholesome

Altheda *See* Althea

Alula *(Arabic)* First

Alura *(Old English)* Divine counsellor

Alva *(Latin)* White

Alvina *(Old English)* Noble companion. *Feminine of* Alvin

Alyce *See* Alice

Alys *See* Alice

Alysia *(Greek)* Possessive/Sane

Alyssa *(Greek)* Sane/rational

Alzena *(Arabic)* Woman

Ama *See* Amabel

Amabel *(Latin)* Lovable

Amabelle *See* Amabel

Amadea *(Latin)* One who is loved of God. *Feminine of* Amadeus

Amadee *See* Amadea

Amanda *(Latin)* Beloved/Lovable

Amandine *(French)* Amanda

Amarina *(Australian Aboriginal)* Rain

Amaris *(Hebrew)* Promise of God

Amaryllis *(Greek)* Fresh

Amata *(Spanish)*
Amanda

Amber *(Arabic)*
Jewel/Light

Ambrosia *(Latin)*
Immortal one

Ambrosine *(Greek)*
Immortal

Amelia *(Old German)*
Industrious

Amelie *(French)* Amelia

Amelinda *(Latin)*
Beloved/Beautiful

Amethyst *(Greek)*
Beneficent

Ami *See* Amy

Amice *(Latin)* Loving

Amie *See* Amy

Aminta *(Latin)* One who
protects

Amity *(Old French)*
Friendship

Amorette *(Latin)*
Dearest

Amy *(French)* Beloved

Anastasia *(Greek)*
Resurrection

Anastasie *(French)*
Anastasia

Anatola *(Greek)* Eastern
woman

Ancelin *(Latin)*
Hand-maiden

Anchoret *(Welsh)*
Beloved

Andrea *(Latin)*
Womanly. *Feminine of
Andrew*

Andreans *See* Andrea

Andri *See* Andrea

Andrial *See* Andrea

Andriana *See* Andrea

Aneira *(Welsh)*
Honorable

Anemone *(Greek)*
Wildflower

Angel *See* Angela

Angela *(Greek)*
Heavenly
messenger/Angel

Angelica *(Latin)* Like
an angel

Angelika *(German)*
Angelica

Angelina *See* Angela

Angeline *See* Angela

Angelique *(French)* Angelica

Angie *See* Angela

Anh *(Vietnamese)* Flower

Anita *(Spanish)* Anne/Ann

Anjelica *See* Angelica

Ann *(Hebrew)* Grace

Anna *(Dutch, German, Scandinavian)* Ann

Annabelle *(Hebrew)* Beautiful woman

Annabla *(Irish)* Annabelle

Annamarie Anna + Maria

Anne *See* Ann

Annette *(French)* Ann

Annie *See* Ann

Annis *(Greek)* One who is complete

Annunciata *(Latin)* Bearer of news

Anthea *(Greek)* Like a flower

Antje *(Dutch)* Anne

Antoinette *(Latin)* Without price

Antonetta *(Swedish)* Antoinette

Antonia *See* Antoinette

Antonie *(German)* Antoinette

Antonietta *(Italian)* Antoinette

Anya *(Hebrew)* Grace

Apanie *(Australian Aboriginal)* Water

Apolline *(Greek)* Sunlight

April *(Latin)* Forthcoming. *Also* the month

Ara *(Greek)* Altar

Arabela *(Spanish)* Arabella

Arabella *(Latin)* Beautiful altar/Entreated

Arabelle *(French)* Arabella

36

Ardath *(Hebrew)* Field of flowers

Ardeen *See* Ardelle

Ardelia *See* Arabella

Ardelle *(Latin)* Ardent

Arden *(Old English)* Valley of eagles

Ardene *See* Arabella

Arella *(Hebrew)* Messenger of God

Areta *(Greek)* Excellent

Aretha *See* Areta

Arette *(French)* Areta

Argenta *(Latin)* Silvery

Aria *(Italian)* Melody

Ariadne *(Greek)* Holy person

Ariel *See* Ariella

Ariella *(Hebrew)* Lioness of God. *Feminine of* Ariel

Ariena *See* Ariella

Ariette *(Italian)* Melody

Arika *(Australian Aboriginal)* Water-lily

Arlene *(Irish)* Pledge

Arleta *See* Ariella

Arlette *See* Ariella

Armilia *(Latin)* Maid who wears a bracelet into battle

Armina *(Old German)* Maiden of war

Arnalda *(Old German)* Strong as an eagle. *Feminine of* Arnold

Arnurna *(Australian Aboriginal)* Blue water lily

Arora *(Australian Aboriginal)* Cockatoo

Aselma *(Gaelic)* Fair one

Ashley *(Anglo-Saxon)* From the ash-tree meadow

Asta *(Greek)* Star

Asteria *(Greek)* Bright star

Astra *(Greek)* Like a star

Astrid *(Norse)* Divine strength

Atalanta *(Greek)* Powerful opponent

Atalaya *(Spanish)*

Guardian

Atalia *See* Athalia

Atara *(Hebrew)* Crown

Atera *See* Atara

Ateret *See* Atara

Athalia *(Hebrew)* God is exalted

Athena *(Greek)* Wisdom

Atlanta *See* Atalanta

Aubine *(French)* Albinia

Aubrey *(Old French)* Ruler

Audrey *(Old English)* Strong/Noble

Audrie *See* Audrey

Audry *See* Audrey

Augusta *(Latin)* Majestic

Aura *(Latin)* Gentle breeze

Aurea *See* Aura

Aurelia *(Latin)* Golden

Aurora *(Latin)* Dawn

Ava *(Latin)* Birdlike

Aveline *See* Evelyn

Avena *(Latin)* Field of oata

Avera *(Hebrew)* Transgressor

Averil *(Old English)* Like a boar

Averyl *See* April

Avice *(Old French)* Warlike

Avis *(Latin)* Bird

Aviva *(Hebrew)* Springtime

Avril *(French)* April

Awena *(Welsh)* Poetry

Ayn *See* Ann

Azalea *(Latin)* Dry earth. *Also* name of a flower

Azaria *(Hebrew)* Blessed

Azelia *(Hebrew)* Assisted by God

Azura *(Old French, Persian)* Blue sky

B

Bab *(Arabic)* From the gateway

Babette *(Greek)* Stranger. *Also diminutive of* Barbara, Elizabeth

Babita *See* Barbara

Baiamul *(Australian Aboriginal)* Black swan

Bakana *(Australian Aboriginal)* Sentinel

Balbina *(Italian)* Little one who stammers

Bambi *(Italian)* Child

Bambra *(Australian Aboriginal)* Mushroom

Baptista *(Latin)* One who baptises

Baptiste *(French)* Batista

Bara *(Australian Aboriginal)* Sunrise

Barbara *(Latin)* Stranger

Barbe *(French)* Barbara

Barbette *See* Barbara

Barbra *See* Barbara

Barite *(Australian Aboriginal)* Girl

Barrandura *(Australian Aboriginal)* Brush myrtle

Basilia *(Greek)* Regal

Bathilda *(Old German)* Maiden in command of a battle

Bathilde *(French)* Bathilda

Bathsheba *(Hebrew)* Seventh daughter

Batista *(Greek)* Baptised

Bautista *(Spanish)* Batista

Bea *See* Beatrice

Beata *(Latin)* Blessed one

Beatrice *(Latin)* One who brings joy

Beatrix *See* Beatrice

Bebe *See* Bibi

Becky *See* Rebecca

Beda *(Old English)*

Warrior maiden

Bee *See* Beatrice

Beeree *(Australian Aboriginal)* Lagoon

Beitris *(Scottish)* Beatrice

Bela *(Czech)* White

Belilanca *(Italian)* Blond

Belinda *(Italian)* Beautiful woman

Belle *(French)* Beautiful

Benedetta *(Italian) See* Benita

Benedikta *(German) See* Benita

Benita *(Latin)* Blessed one

Benoite *(French) See* Benita

Berdine *(Old German)* Bright girl

Berenice *See* Bernice

Bergette *See* Bridget

Bernadette *(French) Feminine of* Bernard

Bernadine *(French)*

Brave as a bear

Bernice *(Greek)* One who brings victory

Bernita *See* Bernadette

Berta *(German, Italian, Spanish)* Bertha

Bertha *(Old English)* Bright

Berthe *(French)* Bertha

Bertilde *(Old English)* Glowing battle maid.

Beryl *(Greek)* Precious sea-green jewel

Bess *See* Elizabeth

Beth *(Hebrew)* House of God. *Short for* Elizabeth

Bethany *(Aramaic)* House of poverty

Betsy *See* Elizabeth

Bette *See* Elizabeth

Bettina *(Italian)* Benedict

Betty *See* Elizabeth

Beulah *(Hebrew)* Married

Beverly *(Old English)* One who lives at the

meadow of beavers

Bevin *(Gaelic)* Melodious woman.

Bianca *(Italian)* White

Bibi *(Arabic)* Lady

Billie *(Old English)* Strong-willed. *Also diminutive of* Wilhelmina

Binnie *See* Belinda

Birgit *See* Bridget

Birgitta *See* Bridget

Bjorg *(Scandinavian)* Salvation

Blair *(Scottish)* Plains dweller

Blake *(Old English)* Swarthy

Blanca *(Spanish)* Belilanca

Blanche *(French)* Fair/White

Blanka *(German)* Blanca

Blinnie *(Irish)* Blanca

Blithe *See* Blythe

Blossom *(Old English)* Like a flower

Blythe *(Old English)* Happy

Bo *(Chinese)* Precious. short for Bonita.

Bobbie *See* Roberta

Bobby *See* Roberta

Bonita *(Spanish)* Pretty

Bonnie *(Latin)* Good

Bonny *(Scottish)* Good/pretty

Boonal *(Australian Aboriginal)* Plentiful grass

Breanne *See* Brianna

Brenda *(Old English)* Firebrand/Fighter

Briana *See* Brianna

Brianna *(Irish)* One who is strong. *Feminine of* Brian.

Brianne *See* Brianna

Bridget *(Celtic)* Strong

Brigitte *See* Bridget

Brita *See* Bridget

Bronwen *(Old Welsh)* White breast

41

Brooke *(Old English)* Stream

Brucie *(Old French)* Feminine of Bruce

Bruna *(Italian)* Brown

Brunelia *(French)* Brown-haired

Brunella *See* Brunelia.

Brunhilda *(Old German)* Heroine

Bryana *See* Brianna

Bryony *(English)* Name of a plant

Buena *(Spanish)* Good

Buffy *See* Elizabeth

Bunny *See* Bernice

C

Cadena *See* Cadence

Cadence *(Latin)* Rhythmic

Cadenza *(Italian)* Cadence

Caera *(Irish)* Ruddy complexion

Caitlin *(Irish)* Catherine

Calandra *(Greek)* Lark

Calandria *(Spanish)* Calandra

Calantha *(Greek)* Beautiful flower

Calca *(Australian Aboriginal)* Star

Caledonia *(Latin)* From Scotland

Calia *(Greek)* Beautiful

Calida *(Spanish)* Ardent

Calista *(Greek)* Very beautiful

Calliope *(Greek)* Beautiful face

Callula *(Latin)* Small beauty

Calypso *(Greek)* One who conceals

Cameo *(Italian)* Sculptured jewel

Camila *(Spanish)* Canille

Camille *(Latin)* Young ceremonial attendant

Cammie *See* Camille

Canace *(Greek)* Daughter of the wind

Candace *(Latin)* Pure/glowing

Candice *See* Candace

Candida *(Latin)* White

Candra *(Latin)* Glowing

Candy *See* Candace

Caprice *(Italian)* Fanciful

Cara *(Italian)* Dearest

Caragh *(Irish)* Love

Carel *See* Caroi

Caresse *(French)* Endearing

Cari *(Turkish)* Flowing like water

Carina *See* Cara

Carine *See* Caragh

Carissa *(Latin)* Dear one

Carita *(Latin)* Charity/Beloved

Carla *See* Caroline

Carleen *(Irish)* Charlotte

Carline *See* Caroline

Carling *(Gaelic)* Little champion

Carlita *See* Caroline

Carlotta *(Italian)* Charlotte

Carly *(German)* Free woman

Carma *(Sanskrit)* Destiny

Carmel *(Hebrew)* God's vineyard or garden

Carmela *(Italian)* Carmel

Carmelita *(Spanish)* Carmel

Carmen *(Latin)* Song

Carmencita *(Spanish)* Carmen

Carmine *See* Carmen

Carmita *See* Carmen

Caroi *(Latin)* Womanly and strong. *Feminine of* Carl

Carol *(Old German)* Song of joy

Carolina *(Spanish)*

Caroline

Caroline *(Old German)* Powerful

Carrie *See* Caragh

Cartin *(Irish)* Catherine

Caryl *(Welsh)* Beloved

Casey *(Irish)* Brave

Cassandra *(Greek)* Confuser of men/Prophetess

Cassidy *(Irish)* Bright/clever one

Cassie *See* Cassandra

Catarina *(Italian)* Catherine

Catherine *(Greek)* Pure/Maidenly

Cathleen *See* Catherine

Catriona *(Gaelic)* Catherine

Cecilia *(Latin)* Dim-sighted. *Feminine of* Cecil

Ceinlys *(Welsh)* Gem

Celene *(Greek)* The moon. *See also* Selene

Celesta *See* Celeste

Celeste *(Latin)* Heavenly

Celia *See* Cecilia

Cerys *(Welsh)* Love

Chandra *(Sanskrit)* Like the moon

Chantal *(French)* Singer

Chantelle *(French)* Little singer

Charita *(Italian)* Charitable

Charity *See* Charita

Charleen *See* Caroline

Charlene *See* Caroline

Charlotta *(Swedish)* Caroline

Charlotte *(Old German)* Woman

Charmaine *(French)* Carmen

Chastity *(Latin)* Chaste/Pure

Chelsea *(English)* A London suburb

Chemarin *(Hebrew)*

Girl wearing black

Chemosh (*Hebrew*) Peacemaker

Chen (*Chinese*) Precious

Cher (*French*) Dear

Chérie (*French*) Darling

Cherise (*Old French*) Cherry-like

Cheryl (*Welsh*) Love

Chesna (*Slavic*) At peace

Chiara (*Italian*) Clare

Chiquita (*Spanish*) Little one

Chlaris *See* Clarissa

Chloe (*Greek*) Fresh young blossom

Chloris (*Greek*) Flower goddess

Chrissa *See* Carissa

Christabel (*Latin/French*) Beautiful Christian

Christina (*French*) Christian

Chryseis (*Latin*)

Daughter of the golden one

Chu (*Chinese*) A pearl

Cicely *See* Cecilia

Cilla *See* Priscilla

Cindy *See* Cynthia

Cissy *See* Cecilia

Claire (*Latin*) Bright

Clara *See* Claire

Clarice *See* Clarissa

Clarinda (*Spanish*) Brilliant

Clarine *See* Claire

Clarissa (*Latin*) Billiant/shining

Claudette (*French*) Claudia

Claudia (*Latin*) Lame. *Feminine of* Claude

Claudine (*French*) Claudia

Cleantha *See* Cliantha

Cleanthe (*French*) Cliantha

Clematis (*Greek*) Vine/brushwood. *Also*

the name of a flower

Clementine (*Greek*) Mercy

Cleo (*Greek*) Famous. *Also diminutive of* Cleopatra

Cleopatra (*Greek*) Father's pride and joy.

Cliantha (*Greek*) Glory-flower

Clio (*Greek*) The proclaimer/Muse of history

Cloe (*Greek*) Glory

Clorinda (*Latin*) Beautiful and famous one

Clorita (*Spanish*) Clare

Clothilde (*French*) Clotilda

Clotilda (*German*) Famous battle-maid

Clover (*Old English*) Clover blossom

Clymene (*Greek*) Famous one

Clytie (*Greek*)

Splendid/beautiful

Cody (*Old English*) Cushion

Colette (*Latin*) Victorious. *Also diminutive of* Nicole

Coline See Columba

Colleen (*Caelic*) Girl

Collette (*French*) Colette

Columba (*Latin*) A dove

Combara (*Australian Aboriginal*) Tomorrow

Conception (*Latin*) Beginning

Conchita (*Spanish*) Conception

Concordia (*Latin*) Harmony

Connie See Constance

Conny See Constance

Consolata (*Italian*) Consolation

Constance (*Latin*) Firmness/Constancy

Constanza (*Italian, Spanish*) Constance

Consuela *(Spanish)* Consolation

Coolalie *(Australian Aboriginal)* South wind

Cora *(Greek)* Maiden

Corabelle *(Greek)* Beautified maiden

Coral *(Latin)* Sincere

Coralie *(French)* Coral

Coraline *See* Coral

Cordelia *(Celtic)* Jewel of the sea

Corey *(Irish)* From the hollow

Corinne *See* Cora

Corissa *(Latin-Greek)* Maidenly

Corliss *(Old English)* Happy, kind-hearted

Cornela *See* Cornelia

Cornelia *(Latin)* Yellow. *Feminine of* Cornelius

Cornelle *See* Cornelia

Corona *(Spanish)* Crowned

Corrie *See* Cora

Cory *See* Cora

Cosetta *(Italian)* Cosette

Cosette *(French)* Victorious

Cosima *(Italian)* Order

Courtney *(Latin)* Short nose

Cressida *(Greek)* Golden one

Crisiant *(Welsh)* Crystal

Crispina *(Latin)* One with curly hair

Crystal *(Latin)* Clear

Cynara *(Greek)* Thistle

Cynthia *(Greek)* The moon

D

Dagmar *(Old German)* Glorious day

Dahna *(Arabic)* Desert

Daisy *(Old English)* Eye of the day

Dale *(Old English)* From

47

the valley

Dallas *(Irish)* Wise

Damaris *(Greek)* Wife

Damita *(Spanish)* Little noble woman

Dana *(Celtic, Scandinavian)* A Dane

Daniela *(Spanish)* Danielle

Danielle *(Hebrew)* Judged by God. *Feminine of* Daniel

Daphne *(Greek)* Laurel tree

Dara *(Hebrew)* House of wisdom

Darcie *(Old French)* Woman from the fortress. *Feminine of* D'Arcy

Daria *(Greek)* Regal/wealthy. *Feminine of* Darius

Darleen *(Old English)* Little darling

Davida *See* Davina

Davina *(Hebrew)*

Beloved

Dawn *(Old English)* Break of day

Dayle *See* Dale

Deanna *See* Diana

Debbie *See* Deborah

Deborah *(Hebrew)* Bee

Debra *See* Deborah

Decima *(Latin)* Tenth daughter

Dee Dee *See* Deirdre

Dee *(Welsh)* Dark one

Deirdre *(Gaelic)* Sorrow

Delfine *(Greek)* Delphinium flower

Delia *(Greek)* Visible/Moon goddess

Delia *See* Cordelia

Délice *See* Delicia

Delicia *(Latin)* Delight

Delma *(Spanish)* Of the sea

Delora *See* Dolores

Delores *See* Dolores

Delphine *See* Delfine

Delta *(Greek)* Fourth daughter

Delvene *See* Delfine

Demetria *(Greek) Feminine of* Demetrios

Dena *(Old English)* From the valley

Denise *(French)* Follower of Dionysus, the god of wine/Wine goddess

Desdemona *(Greek)* Unlucky

Désirée *(French)* Desired

Desma *(Greek)* Pledge

Desmona *See* Desdemona

Deva *(Sanskrit)* Divine

Dextra *(Latin)* Skillful

Diamanta *(French)* Like a diamond

Diana *(Latin)* Goddess of the moon

Diane *See* Diana

Dianne *See* Diana

Diantha *(Greek)* Divine flower

Dianthia *See* Diantha

Didi *See* Deirdre

Dina *(Hebrew)* Judged/Vindicated

Dinah *See* Dina

Dixie *(Latin)* Tenth/Girl from the Southern States of America

Doanna Dorothy+Anna

Docila *(Latin)* Docile/gentle

Dolly *See* Doreen/Dorothy

Dolores *(Latin)* Lady of Sorrows

Domenico *(Italian)* Dominique

Domina *(Latin)* Lady

Dominique *(French)* Belonging to the Lord

Donalda *(Gaelic) Feminine of* Donald

Donata *(Latin)* Gift

Donna *(Latin)* Noble lady

Dora *(Greek)* Gift. *See also* Theodora

Dorcas *(Greek)* Gazelle

Doreen *(Irish)* Sullen/Moody

Dorinda *(Greek)* Beautiful gift

Doris *(Greek)* From the ocean/Sea goddess

Dorotea *(Italian)* Dorothy

Dorothea *See* Dorothy

Dorothy *(Greek)* Gift of God

Dorrie *See* Dora

Drusilla *(Latin)* Strong one

Duana *(Irish)* Little dark one

Duena *(Spanish)* Chaperon

Dulciana *See* Dulcie

Dulcibelle *See* Dulcie

Dulcie *(Latin)* Sweet/Charming

Durene *(Latin)* One who endures

Dwana *See* Duana

Dymphia *(Latin)* Nurse

Dymphna *(Irish)* Eligible/Befitting

Dysis *(Greek)* Sunset

E

Earlene *(Old English)* Noble woman. *Feminine of* Earl

Earline *See* Earlene

Eartha *(Old English)* Child of the earth/Earth

Easter *(Old English)* One born at Easter

Ebba *(Old English)* Retreating tide

Ebony *(Greek)* Black wood

Echo *(Greek)* Reflected sound

Eda *(Old English)* Poetry/Happy

Edana *(Irish)* Little fiery one

Edda *(Old Norse)* Poetry

Edina *(Scottish)* From Edinburgh. *See* also Edwina

Edita *(Italian)* Edith

Edith *(Old English)* Rich gift

Ediva *See* Edith

Edlyn *(Old English)* Noble/prosperous little one

Edmonda *(Old English)* Prosperous protector. *Feminine of* **Edmund**

Edna *(Hebrew)* Rejuvenation

Edra *See* Edrea

Edrea *(Old English)* Prosperous/powerful

Edwardine *(Old English)* Prosperous guardian. *Feminine of* Edward

Edwina *(Old English)* Rich and happy friend. *Feminine of* Edwin

Effie *(Greek)* Highly regarded

Egberta *(Old English)* Shining sword. *Feminine of* Egbert

Egbertina *See* Egberta

Egilantine *(Old French)* Sweet brier rose

Eileen *(Irish)* Helen

Einore *See* Eleanore

Eir *(Old Norse)* Healer

Eivena *See* Alvina

Eivina *See* Alvina

Ekaterina *(Russian)* Catherine

Elaine *(Old French)* Helen

Elanora *(Australian Aboriginal)* Seashore

Elberta *See* Alberta

Eldora *(Spanish)* Golden

Eldrida *(Old English)* Wise counsellor. *Feminine of* Eldred

Eleanor *(Greek)* Light

Electra *(Greek)*

Brilliant/Shining

Eleebana *(Australian Aboriginal)* Beautiful girl

Elena *(Italian/Spanish)* Helen

Eleni *(Greek)* Helen

Elenore *(German)* Eleanor

Eleonore *See* Eleanor

Elfreda *See* Elfrida

Elfrida *(Old English)* Wise and peaceful one

Elga *(Slavic)* Holy

Elinor *See* Eleanor

Elinore *See* Eleanor

Elise *(French)* Elizabeth

Elissa *See* Elizabeth

Eliza *See* Elizabeth

Elizabeth *(Hebrew)* Consecrated to God

Ella *(Old English)* Elf

Ellen *(Scottish)* Helen

Ellie *Diminutive of* Elizabeth

Ellie *See* Alice

Ellinore *(Danish)* Helen

Ellis *(Irish)* Elizabeth

Elmira *(Old English)* Noble

Eloise *(Old German)* Healthy

Elsa *(Old German)* Noble. *See also* Alice. *Also diminutive of* Elizabeth

Elsie *(Hebrew)* Noble. *Also diminutive of* Elizabeth and Elsa

Elspeth *(Scottish)* Elizabeth

Elva *See* Alfreda

Emily *(Gothic)* Industrious

Emma *(Old German)* Universal/All embracing

Emmanuela *(Hebrew)* God with us

Emmylou *(American)* *From* Emma + Louise

Emogene *See* Imogen

Endota *(Australian Aboriginal)* Beautiful

52

Engracia *(Spanish)* Grace

Enid *(Irish)* Purity

Ennea *(Greek)* Ninth daughter

Enrica *(Italian) Feminine of* Henry

Eolande *See* Yolande

Eranthe *(Greek)* Spring flower

Erda *See* Eartha

Erica *(Norse)* Powerful/Ruler. *Feminine of* Eric

Erin *(Irish)* Peace. *Also* another name for Ireland

Erma *See* Irma

Ermine *(Latin)* Regal

Erna *(Old English)* Eagle

Ernestine *(Old English)* Earnest one. *Feminine of* Ernest

Erwina *(Old English)* Friend from the sea

Esmé *(French)* Gracious protector

Esmeralda *(Spanish)* Emerald

Essie *Diminutive of* Esther

Esta *(Italian)* One from the East

Estelle *(French)* Star

Esther *(Hebrew)* Star

Eswen *(Welsh)* Strength

Ethel *(Old English)* Noble

Ethelinda *(Old German)* Noble serpent

Etta *(Old German)* Little. *Also diminutive of* Henrietta

Eudice *See* Judith

Eudocia *(Greek)* Honoured

Eudora *(Greek)* Happy gift

Eugenia *(Greek)* Nobly born

Eulalia *(Greek)* One who speaks well

Eulalie *(French)* Eulalia

Eunice *(Greek)* Happy/Victorious

Euphemia *(Greek)*
Good repute

Eurwen *(Welsh)*
Golden/Fair

Eustacia *(Latin)*
Fruitful. *Feminine of
Eustace*

Eva *See* Eve

Evadne *(Greek)* One
who sings sweetly

Evaleen *See* Eve

Evangeline *(Greek)*
Bearer of good news

Eve *(Hebrew)* Life-giving

Eveline *See* Evelyn

Evelyn *(Old German)*
Hazelnut

Evita *See* Eve

Evlyn *See* Evelyn

Evonne *See* Yvonne

Eydie *See* Edith

F

Fabia *(Latin)* Bean
grower

Fae *See* Fay

Faina *See* Faine

Faine *(Old English)*
Joyful

Faith *(Latin)*
Trust/Loyalty

Faizah *(Arabic)*
Victorious

Fanchon *(French)* Free

Fanny *See* Frances

Farica *See* Frederica

Farrah *(Arabic)*
Happiness

Fatima *(Arabic)* Name
of Muhammad's
daughter

Fatimah *See* Fatima

Fatma *See* Fatima

Favor *(Old French)* One
who helps

Fawn *(French)* Young deer

Fay *(French)* Fairy

Fayanne Fay+Anne

Faye *See* Fay

Fayette *(French)* Fay

Fedora *See* Theodora

Felice *(Latin)* Happy

Felicia *(Italian)* Happy

Feliciana *(Spanish)* Felice

Felicity *See* Felicia. *Feminine of* Felix

Felipa *(Spanish)* Philippa

Felise *(French)* Happy

Fenella *(Irish)* White-shouldered

Fern *(Old English)* Feather

Fernanda *(Gothic)* Adventurous. *Feminine of* Ferdinand

Fidelia *See* Fidelity

Fidelity *(Latin)* Faithful

Fifi *(French) Diminutive of* Josephine

Filipa *See* Philippa

Filippa *(Italian)* Philippa

Filma *(Old English)* Veiled

Finola *(Irish) See* Fenella

Fiona *(Irish)* Fair one

Flavia *(Latin)* Blonde

Fleur *(French)* Flower

Fleurette *(French)* Little flower

Flo *See* Flora/Florence

Flora *(Latin)* Flower. *Also diminutive of* Florence

Florence *(Latin)* Blooming

Florimel *(Greek)* Nectar

Florine *See* Florence

Floris *See* Florence

Fonda *(Middle English)* Affectionate one

Frances *(Latin)* Free

Francesca *(Italian)* Frances

Françoise *(French)* Frances

Francyne *See* Frances

Frankie *See* Frances

Freda *(Old German)* Peaceful. *Also see* Alfreda, Wilfreda

Frederica *(Old German)* Peaceful ruler

Freida *See* Wilfreda

Freya *(Old Norse)* Noble woman. *Also* the name of a goddess

Frieda *See* Freda

Fulvia *(Latin)* Blonde

G

Gabrielle *(Hebrew)* God is my strength. *Feminine of* Gabriel

Gaby *Diminutive of* Gabrielle

Gae *See* Gay

Gaea *(Greek)* The earth

Gai *(Old French)* Lively

Gail *(Old English)* Lively

Gala *See* Gaea

Galatea *(Greek)* White/Milky

Gale *(Old Norse)* Singer

Gardenia *(Latin)* White flower

Garland *(French)* Garland of flowers

Garnet *(Middle English)* Dark red

Gasparde *(French)* *Feminine of* Gasper

Gavrila *(Hebrew)* Heroine. *Feminine of* Gabriel

Gay *(French)* Lighthearted

Gayle *See* Gail

Gazelle *(Arabic)* Small antelope

Gemma *(Italian)* Gem

Gene *See* Eugenia

Geneva *(Old French)* Juniper tree

Genevieve *(French)* White wave

Genie *See* Eudice

Georgene *See* Georgia

Georgette *(French)*
Georgia

Georgia *(Greek)* Farm
girl

Georgina *See* Georgia

Georgine *See* Georgia

Geraldine *(Old
German)* Noble spear
carrier

Geranium *(Greek)*
Geranium (the flower)

Gerda *(Old German)*
Protected one. *Short for*
Gertrude

Germaine *(French)*
Protector

Gertrude *(Old German)*
Woman warrior

Gertrudis *(Spanish)*
Gertrude

Giacinta *(Italian)*
Hyacinth

Gianina *(Italian)* God is
gracious. *Feminine of*
Giovanni

Gigi *See* Virginia

Gilah *(Hebrew)* Joy

Gilberta *(Old German)*
Bright pledge. *Feminine
of* Gilbert

Gilda *(Irish)* God's
servant

Gillian *(Latin)* Young
bird

Gina *See*
Regina/Eugenia

Ginette *(French)*
Genevieve

Ginevra *See* Guinevere

Ginger *(Latin)* Ginger
spice or flower

Giorgia *(Italian)* Georgia

Giorsal *(Scottish)* Grace

Giovanna *(Italian)* Jane

Gipsy *(Old English)*
Wanderer

Giraida *(Italian)* Georgia

Girraween *(Australian
Aboriginal)* Floral place

Gisela *(Old German)*
Pledge

Giselle *See* Gisela

Gita *(Sanskrit)* Song

Gitana *(Spanish)* Gypsy

Githa *(Greek)* Good

Gittel *(Yiddish)* Good

Giulia *(Italian)* Julia

Giustina *(Italian)* Justine

Gladys *(Irish)* Princess

Gleda *(Old English)* Fragile flower

Glenda *(Welsh)* Valley. *Feminine of* Glen

Glenys *(Welsh)* Holy

Gloria *(Latin)* Glory

Gloriana *See* Gloria

Godiva *(Old English)* God's gift

Golda *(Old English)* Gold

Goldie *(Old English)* Golden

Goolcoola *(Australian Aboriginal)* Sweet

Grace *(Latin)* Graceful

Grazia *(Italian)* Grace

Gregoria *(Latin)* Watchful

Greta *See* Margaret

Gretchen *(German)* Margaret

Gretel *(Swiss)* Little Margaret

Griselda *(Old German)* Gray-haired woman warrior

Guenna *See* Gwendolyn

Guglielma *(Italian)* Wilhelmina

Guida *(Italian)* Guide

Guilietta *(Italian)* Julia

Guilla *See* Wilhelmina

Guillelmina *(Spanish)* Wilhelmina

Guillemette *(French)* Wilhelmina

Guinevere *(Welsh)* White/Fair

Guiseppina *(Italian)* Josephine

Gunhilda *(Old Norse)* Battlemaid

Gurley *(Australian Aboriginal)* Willow

Gustava *(Swedish)* Staff of the Goths. *Feminine of*

Gustaf.

Gwen *(Irish)* White. *Also short for* Gwendolyn and Guinevere

Gwenda *See* Gwendolyn

Gwendelen *See* Gwendolyn

Gwendolin *See* Gwendolyn

Gwendoline *See* Gwendolyn

Gwendolyn *(Irish)* White-browed

Gwendydd *(Welsh)* Morning star

Gwenonwyn *(Welsh)* Lily of the valley

Gwyneth *(Irish)* Blessed

H

Hagar *(Hebrew)* Forsaken

Haidee *(Greek)* Modest

Halcyon *(Greek)* Peaceful/Kingfisher

Haley *(Old English)* Ingenious

Haley *See* Haley

Halfrida *(Old German)* Peaceful heroine

Halimeda *(Greek)* One who thinks of the sea

Halla *(Swahili)* Unexpected gift

Hallie *(Greek)* Thinking of the sea

Hana *(Japanese)* Flower

Hanifah *(Arabic)* True believer

Hanna *See* Hannah

Hannah *(Hebrew)* Grace

Hannie *See* Hannah

Hanya *(Australian Aboriginal)* Stone

Hao *(Vietnamese)* Good/Tasteful

Harmonia *(Greek)* Unity

Harmony *See* Harmonia

Harriet *See* Henrietta

Hattie *See* Henrietta

Hatty *See* Henrietta

Hayley *(Old English)* High clearing

Hazel *(Old English)* Hazel-nut tree

Heather *(Middle English)* Flower of the moors/Heavenly rose

Hebe *(Greek)* Youth

Hedda *(Old German)* War

Heddy *See* Hedda

Hedwig *(Old German)* Strife

Hedy *(Greek)* Pleasant

Heidi *(German)* Maid of battle. *Also short for* Adelheid

Helen *(Greek)* Light

Helena *See* Helen

Hélène *See* Helen

Helenka *(Polish)* Helen

Helga *(Old German)* Pious. *Also short for* Olga

Helianthe *(Greek)* Bright flower

Helice *(Greek)* Spiral

Helma *(Old German)* Helmet. *Short for* Wilhelmina

Heloise *(French)* Louise/Eloise

Henrietta *(Old French)* Ruler of the home. *Feminine of* Harry

Henriette *See* Henrietta

Hera *(Greek)* Heavenly queen

Hermia *See* Hermione

Hermina *See* Hermione

Hermine *See* Hermione

Hermione *(Greek)* The daughter of the earth

Hermosa *(Spanish)* Beautiful

Herta *See* Eartha

Hertha *(Old English)* Earth

Hesper *(Greek)* Evening star

Hester *See* Esther

Hettie *See* Henrietta

Hibernia *(Latin)* Ireland

Hilary *(Greek)* Cheerful

Hilda *(Old German)* Female warrior. *Also short for* Hildegarde

Hildegarde *(Old German)* Fortress

Hildreth *(Old German)* Battle counsellor

Hilma *See* Helma

Hine-Hauone *(Polynesian)* Girl made from earth. *Equivalent of Biblical* Eve

Hine-Raumati *(Polynesian)* Mermaid

Hine-Titame *(Polynesian)* Daybreak

Hine *(Polynesian)* Girl

Hiriko *(Japanese)* Generous

Hiriwa *(Polynesian)* Silver

Hoa *(Vietnamese)* Blossom/Flower

Holda *(Old German)* Beloved

Hollie *See* Holly

Holly *(Old English)* One who brings luck

Honey *(Old English)* Sweet one

Hong Ngoc *(Vietnamese)* Ruby

Hong *(Chinese)* Pink

Honora *(Latin)* Honorable

Hope *(Old English)* Hope

Hortense *(Latin)* Garden/Gardener

Hoshi *(Japanese)* Star

Huberta *(Old German)* Brilliant thinker. *Feminine of* Hubert

Hue-Lan *(Vietnamese)* Sweet-smelling orchid

Hulda *(Old German)* Gracious woman

Hyacinth *(Greek)* Hyacinth flower

Hypatia *(Greek)* Highest

I

Ida (*Old English*)
Prosperous/Happy

Idris (*Welsh*) Fiery lord

Ignacia (*Latin*) Ardent.
Feminine of Ignatius

Ila (*Old French*) Island

Ilana (*Hebrew*) Big tree

Ilaria (*Russian*) Hilary

Ileana *See* Iliana

Iliana (*Russian*) Helena

Ilka (*Slavic*) Flattering

Ilona (*Hungarian*)
Beautiful

Ilsa *See* Ailsa

Ilse (*German*) Helen

Imelda (*Latin*) Wishful

Imogen (*Latin*) Image

Imogene *See* Imogen

Ina (*Polynesian*) Name
from mythology

Inas (*Polynesian*) Wife of
the moon

Indira (*Sanskrit*) One of
the names of the
goddess Lakshmi

Indrani (*Sanskrit*) Wife
of Indra, god of the air

Ines (*Spanish*) Agnes

Inez (*Spanish*) Agnes

Inga (*Scandinavian*)
Ingrid

Ingar (*Australian
Aboriginal*) Crayfish

Inge *See* Ingrid

Ingrid (*Norse*) Daughter
of a hero

Iniga (*Latin*) Ardent

Iola (*Greek*) Dawn
cloud/Violet (colour)

Iolanthe (*Greek*) Violet
(*flower*)

Iona (*Australian
Aboriginal*) Fire

Ione (*Greek*)
Violet-coloured stone

Iphigenia (*Greek*)
Sacrifice

Iphigenie *See* Iphigenia

Ira *(Hebrew)* Watchful

Irene *(Greek)* Peace

Iris *(Greek)* Rainbow

Irma *(Latin)* Noble

Isa *(Old German)* Iron-willed

Isabel *(Old Spanish)* Consecrated to God

Isabelle *(French)* Isabel

Isabeu *(Spanish)* Consecrated to God

Isadora *(Greek)* Gift of Isis

Isis *(Egyptian)* Supreme goddess/Goddess of fertility

Isleen *(English)* Aislinn

Isobel *(Scottish)* Isabel

Isola *(Italian)* Island

Isolde *(Welsh)* Fair lady

Ita *(Gaelic)* Thirsting for truth

Ivy *(Old English)* Ivy vine

J

Jacinda *(Greek)* Beautiful

Jacinta *See* Hyacinth

Jackie *See* Jacqueline

Jaclyn *See* Jacqueline

Jacoba *(Latin)* One who supplants. *Feminine of* James/Jacob

Jacqueline *(Hebrew)* One who supplants

Jade *(Spanish)* Jade/Daughter

Jaime *(French)* I love

Jamila *(Arabic)* Beautiful

Jana *(Irish)* Jane

Jane *(Hebrew)* God's gift. *Feminine of* John

Janelle Jane+Ellen

Janet *Diminutive of* Jane

Janice *See* Jane

Janina *See* Jane

Janine *See* Jane

Janna *(Arabic)* Fruit harvest

Jardena *(Hebrew)* Flowing downward. *Feminine of* Jordan

Jarmila *(Slavic)* Spring

Jarnila *(Arabic)* Beautiful

Jasmin *(Persian)* Name of the flower

Jasmine *See* Jasmin

Jayne *(Sanskrit)* Victorious

Jean *(Scottish)* Jane

Jeanne *See* Jean

Jeannette *(French) Diminutive of* Jean

Jeannie *See* Jean

Jemima *(Hebrew)* Dove

Jemina *See* Jemima

Jennifer *(Welsh)* Fair

Jenny *See* Jennifer

Jessica *(Hebrew)* Rich one. *Feminine of* Jesse

Jewel *(Latin)* Precious

Jezebel *(Hebrew)* Impure

Jill *See* Gillian

Jinchilla *(Australian Aboriginal)* Cypress tree

Jo *See* Josephine

Joan *(Hebrew)* God is gracious. *Feminine of* John

Joane Joan + Anne

Jocelyn *(Latin)* Merry/Fair

Jocelyne *See* Jocelyn

Jodi *See* Joan

Jody *See* Joan

Joelle *(Hebrew)* God is willing. *Also feminine of* Joel

Johanna *(German)* Joan

Jolie *(French)* Pretty

Jonquil *(Latin)* Name of the flower

Jordana *(Hebrew)* Descending. *Feminine of* Jordan

Joscelyn *See* Jocelyn

Josephine *(Hebrew)*
You shall multiply. *Also
feminine of* Joseph

Joy *(Latin)* Joyful

Joyce *(French) See* Joy

Juanita *(Spanish)*
Joan/Jane

Judith *(Hebrew)*
Admired/Praised

Judy *See* Judith

Julia *(Latin)* Youthful
one. *Also feminine of*
Julius

Julianne Julie + Anne

Juliet *See* Julia

Julieta *(Spanish)* Julia

Juliette *(French)* Julia

June *(Latin)* Summer's
child. *Also* the month

Junee *(Australian
Aboriginal)* Talk to me

Junella June+Ella

Junette *See* June

Juniata *See* June

Junine *See* June

Juno *(Latin)* Heavenly
one/Queen of heaven

Justine *(Latin)* Just.
Feminine of Justin

Jytte *(Danish)* Judith

K

Kaatje *(Dutch)*
Katherine

Kadla *(Australian
Aboriginal)* Sweet

Kajsa *(Scandinavian)*
Katherine

Kala *(Hindi)* Black

Kali *(Sanskrit)* Energy.
Also name for goddess
Shakti

Kalila *(Arabic)*
Beloved/Darling

Kalinda *(Australian
Aboriginal)* View

Kama *(Sanskrit)* Love

Kamaria *(African)* Like
the moon

Kameko *(Japanese)*
Child of the tortoise

Kamilah *(Arabic)* Perfect one

Kanya *(Sanskrit)* Maiden

Kaooroo *(Australian Aboriginal)* Waterlily

Kara *See* Cara

Karen *(Greek)* Maiden/Virgin. *Also (Scandinavian)* Katherine

Karin *See* Karen

Karla *(German)* Caroline

Karlene *See* Caroline

Karlotte *(German)* Caroline

Karolina *(Polish)* Caroline

Karoline *See* Caroline

Karri *(Australian Aboriginal)* Eucalypt tree

Karston *(Danish)* Christine

Kasmira *(Old Slavic)* One who commands peace

Kassia *(Polish)* Catherine

Kate *Short for* Katherine

Katherine *(Greek)* Pure

Kathleen *(Irish)* Katherine

Kathlin *See* Kathleen

Kathrina *(Danish)* Katherine

Kathryn *See* Katherine

Katie *See* Katherine

Katina *(Australian Aboriginal)* First child

Katinka *(Slavic)* Catherine

Katja *(Russian)* Katherine

Katleen *See* Kathleen

Katlin *See* Kathleen

Katri *(Scandinavian)* Catherine

Kay *(Greek)* Rejoice. *Also short for* Catherine

Kaye *See* Kay

Kaylyn Kay + Lyn

Keely *(Irish)* Beautiful

Keiko *(Japanese)* Adored

Kelda *(Old Norse)* A spring

Kelilah *(Hebrew)* Victory

Kelly *(Irish)* Woman warrior

Kelsey *(Scandinavian)* From the ship

Kendra *(Old English)* One who is knowledgeable

Kerry *(Gaelic)* Dark one

Kesia *(African)* Favourite

Ketti *See* Catherine

Ketura *(Hebrew)* Fragrance

Kiah *(African)* Beginning of the season

Kilkie *(Australian Aboriginal)* Waterhen

Killara *(Australian Aboriginal)* One who is always there

Kim *(Old English)* Chief

Kimberley *(Old English)* From the royal place

Kindilan *(Australian Aboriginal)* Full of joy

Kineta *(Greek)* Active

Kiona *(American Indian)* Brown hills

Kip *(Old English)* From the pointed hill

Kipp *See* Kip

Kira *(Australian Aboriginal)* Fireplace

Kirby *(Old English)* From the church town

Kiri *(Polynesian)* Tree bark

Kirima *(Eskimo)* Hill

Kirra *(Australian Aboriginal)* Leaf

Kirsten *(Norse)* Annointed

Kirstie *See* Kirsten

Kirsty *See* Kirsten

Kitty *See* Katherine

Klara *(German)* Clare

Kohia *(Polynesian)* Passion flower

Kolora *(Australian Aboriginal)* Freshwater lagoon

Konstanze *(German)* Constance

Koo *Short for* Katherine

Kora *(Greek)* Maiden

Kordula *(German)* Cordelia

Koren *(Greek)* Maiden

Kristen *(Scandinavian)* Christine

Kristin *See* Kristen

Kuei *(Chinese)* Very beautiful girl

Kumbelin *(Australian Aboriginal)* Sweetness

Kunama *(Australian Aboriginal)* Snow

Kyle *(Irish)* Good looking

Kylie *(Australian Aboriginal)* Boomerang

Kyna *(Welsh)* Wise

L

Labhaoise *(Irish)* Louise

Laetitia *(Latin)* Joy

Lakkari *(Australian Aboriginal)* Honeysuckle tree

Lala *(Slavic)* Tulip

Lalage *(Greek)* One who speeks freely

Lalita *(Sanskrit)* Direct/Straightforward

Lan *(Vietnamese)* Orchid

Lana *(French)* Climbing vine

Lanelle *(Old French)* Little lane

Lani *(Hawaiian)* Heaven

Lann *(Irish)* Blade

Lanna *See* Helen

Lara *(Latin)* Famous

Laraine *(Latin)* Seagull

Larentia *(Latin)* Foster mother

Larine *(Latin)* Girl from the sea

Larissa *(Greek)* Cheerful

Lark *(English)* Skylark

Lass *(Gaelic)* Young girl

Lassie *Diminutive of* Lass

Lateefa *(Arabic)* Gentle lioness

Laura *(Latin)* Crown of laurel leaves. *Feminine of* Lawrence

Lauren *See* Laura

Lauretta *See* Laura

Laurie *See* Laura

Laveda *(Latin)* Purified

Lavelle *(Latin)* Cleansing

Lavender *(Latin)* Sweet smelling flower

Laverne *(Latin)* Like a spring

Lavette *See* Laveda

Lavinia *(Latin)* Purified

Layaleeta *(Australian Aboriginal)* The ocean

Layla *(Swahili)* Born at night

Lea *See* Leah

Leah *(Hebrew)* Weary

Leala *(Old French)* Faithful

Leana *See* Liana

Leandra *(Latin)* Like a lioness

Leanne *(French)* To bind

Leanor *(Spanish)* Eleanore

Leatrice Leah+Beatrice

Leda *(Greek)* Slim lady

Lee *(Old English)* Meadow

Leena *(Australian Aboriginal)* Water

Leigh *(Old English)* One who lives at the meadow. *See also* Leah

Leila *(Arabic)* Dark as night

Leilani *(Hawaiian)* Heavenly flower

Lela *See* Leila

Lemuela *(Hebrew)* Devoted to God

Lena *(Latin)* Alluring. *Also diminutive of* Helena

Lenis *(Latin)* Smooth

Lenita *(Latin)* Gentle

Lenora *See* Helen

Lenore *See* Eleanor

Leoda *(Old German)* Woman of the people

Leola *(Latin)* Lioness. *Feminine of* Leo.

Leolina *(Welsh)* *Feminine of* Llewelyn

Leoline *See* Liana

Leoma *(Old English)* Light/bright

Leona *(French)* Lion. *Feminine of* Leo

Leonarda *(Spanish)* Brave as a lion

Leone *See* Leona

Leonelle *See* Leona

Leonida *(Russian)* Leona

Leonie *See* Leona

Leonora *See* Eleanor

Leonore *See* Eleanor

Leontine *(Latin)* Like a lion

Leopoldine *(Old German)* Bold for the nation

Leota *See* Leoda

Leotie *(American Indian)* Prairie flower

Lesley *(Irish)* Grey fortress

Leslie *See* Lesley

Letitia *See* Laetitia

Letizia *(Italian)* Laetitia

Leura *(Australian Aboriginal)* Lava

Levanna *(Latin)* Morning sun

Levina

Levina *(Latin)* Lightning. Also *(Hebrew) feminine of* Levi

Lewanna *(Hebrew)* Bright white moon

Lexi *See* Alexandra

Lexine *See* Alexandra

Lian *(Chinese)* Graceful willow

Liana *(French)* To bind

Libby *See* Elizabeth

Liberty *(Latin)* Freedom

Libusa *(Russian)* Darling

Lida *(Slavic)* Beloved of the people

Liesel *See* Liesl

Liesl *(German)* Elizabeth

Lilac *(Persian)* Lilac flower

Lilian *See* Lillian

Lilibet *See* Elizabeth *(Family nickname for Queen Elizabeth II)*

Lilith *(Arabic)* Of the night

Lillian *(Latin)* Lily

Linda *(Spanish)* Pretty one. *Also short for* Belinda

Lindall *(Old English)* From the dale

Linden *(Old English)* Shield

Lindsay *(Old English)* From the linden tree island

Lindsey *See* Lindsay

Lindy *See* Linda

Linette *(Irish)* Graceful

Lira *(Australian Aboriginal)* River

Lirralirra *(Australian Aboriginal)* Wren

Lisa *See* Elizabeth

Lisbeth *See* Elizabeth

Lisha *(Arabic)* Darkness before midnight

Liusadh *(Scottish)* Louise

Liz *See* Elizabeth

Liza *See* Elizabeth

Loella *See* Luella

Lois *(Greek)* Pleasing

Lola *(Spanish)* Strong woman. *Also diminutive of* Dolores

Lolita *Diminutive of* Lola

Lomasi *(American Indian)* Pretty flower

Lona *(Middle English)* Solitary

Lorelei *(German)* Alluring

Lorelle *(Latin)* Little

Loren *See* Laura

Loretta *See* Laura

Lorna *See* Laura

Lorraine *(Old German)*

71

Famous warrior

Lotta *See* Charlotte

Lotte *See* Charlotte

Lotus *(Greek)* Lotus flower

Louanna *See* Luana

Louella *See* Luella

Louisa *See* Louise

Louise *(Old German)* Famous woman warrior. *Feminine of* Louis

Loyce *See* Louise

Luana *(Hebrew)* Graceful woman warrior

Lucerne *(Latin)* Circle of light

Lucette *See* Lucille

Lucia *(Italian)* Lucille

Lucianna *(Italian)* Lucy+Anne

Lucie *(German)* Lucille

Lucienne *(French)* Lucille

Lucille *(French)* Lucy

Lucinda Lucy + Linda

Lucita *(Spanish)* Mary of the light

Lucrecia *(Spanish)* Lucretia

Lucretia *(Latin)* Reward/wealth

Lucrezia *(Italian)* Lucretia

Lucy *(Latin)* Light. *Feminine of* Lucius

Ludelia *See* Luella

Ludmilla *(Slavic)* Beloved of the people

Ludovika *(German)* Louise

Luella *(Old English)* Renowned elf

Luighseach *(Irish)* Lucille

Luisa *(Italian/Spanish)* Louise

Lulu *See* Louise

Lunetta *(Italian)* Little moon

Lupe *(Latin)* Wolf

Lurette *See* Lorelei

Luriene *See* Lorelei

Lurline *See* Lorelei

Luwana *See* Luana

Luz *(Spanish)* Lucille

Lydia *(Greek)* Beautiful/Woman from the country Lydia

Lynda *See* Linda

Lynette *(Welsh)* Idol

Lynne *(Old English)* Pool

Lyris *(Greek)* One who plays the lyre

Lysandra *(Greek)* Liberator

M

Mab *(Gaelic)* Joy/Queen of the fairies. *See also* Amabel

Mabel *(Latin)* Lovable

Mabelle *(French)* Mabel

Macaria *(Greek)* Happy

Madalena *See* Madeleine

Maddalena *(Italian)* Madeleine

Madel *See* Madeleine

Madeleine *(Greek)* Tower of strength/Magnificent

Madeline *See* Madeleine

Madelle *See* Madeleine

Madelon *See* Madeleine

Madge *See* Margaret

Madlen *See* Madeleine

Madlin *See* Madeleine

Madonna *(Latin)* My lady

Madra *(Spanish)* Mother

Mae *See* May

Magda *(German)* Madeleine

Magdala *See* Madeleine

Magdalene *See* Madeleine

Maggy *See* Margaret

Magnilda *(German)* Mild, gentle one

Magnolia *(Latin)* Magnolia plant

Mahalia *(Hebrew)*

Tenderness

Maia *(Greek)* Mother

Maible *(Irish)* Mabel

Maida *(Old English)* Maiden

Maisie *See* Margaret

Malina *See* Madeleine

Malinda *(Greek)* Gentle

Malva *(Greek)* Tender

Malvina *See* Melvina

Manda *See* Amanda

Mandal *See* Amanda

Mandaline *See* Amanda

Mandisa *(Xhosa)* Sweet

Mandy *See* Amanda

Mansi *(Hopi Indian)* Plucked flower

Manuela *(Spanish)* God is with us

Mara *(Hebrew)* Bitter

Marcela *(Spanish)* Marcella

Marcella *(Latin)* Warlike one. *Feminine of* Marcus

Marcellina *See* Marcella

Marcia *(Latin)* Warlike

Marcie *See* Marcia

Marcille *See* Marcella

Maree *See* Mary

Marelda *(Old German)* Famous woman warrior

Marga *See* Margaret

Margaret *(Greek)* Pearl

Margaretha *(Dutch)* Margaret

Margarette *See* Margaret

Margarita *See* Margaret

Margaux *(French)* Margaret

Marge *See* Margaret

Margery *See* Margaret

Margherita *(Italian)* Margaret

Margie *See* Margaret

Margo *See* Margaret

Margot *(French)* Margaret

Margreth *(Danish)* Margaret

Marguerite *(French)*

Margaret

Maria *See* Mary

Mariah *See* Mary

Marian *See* Marion

Mariana *(Spanish)* Marion

Marianna *(Italian)* Marion

Marianne *(French)* Marion

Marianne *(German)* Marion

Marie *(French)* Mary

Mariette *See* Mary

Marigold *(Old English)* Mary's gold

Marika *See* Mary

Marilyn *See* Mary

Marina *(Latin)* From the sea

Marion *(Hebrew)* Sea of bitterness

Marisa *See* Marina

Marjory *See* Margaret

Marlene *See* Madeleine

Marnie *See* Marina

Marsha *See* Marcia

Martha *(Arabic)* Lady

Martina *(Latin)* Warlike

Mary *(Hebrew)* Bitter

Maryanne Mary + Anne

Marybeth Mary + Beth

Maryellen Mary + Ellen

Maryjo Mary + Joanne

Marylin *See* Mary

Marylou Mary+ Louise

Mathilda *(Old German)* Powerful woman warrior

Matilda *See* Mathilda

Mattie *See* Mathilda

Maude *See* Mathilda

Maura *(Irish)* Mary

Maureen *(Irish)* Little Mary

Mave *See* Mab

Mavis *(French)* Thrush

Maxine *(Latin)* Greatest

May *(Latin)* Great

Maybelle *See* Mabel

75

Mayra *(Australian Aboriginal)* Spring wind

Meara *(Gaelic)* Laughter/Mirth

Meave See Mab

Medwenna *(Welsh)* Maiden

Meg See Margaret

Megan *(Irish)* Strong

Mei *(Chinese)* Beautiful

Melanie *(Greek)* Black

Melantha *(Greek)* Dark flower

Melany See Melanie

Melba *(Greek)* Soft

Melina *(Greek)* Song

Melisande *(French)* Melissa/Millicent

Melisenda *(Spanish)* Millicent

Melissa *(Greek)* Honey bee

Melita *(Italian)* Melissa

Melodie See Melody

Melody *(Greek)* Song

Melvina *(Irish)* Like a chief. *Feminine of* Melvin

Menorah *(Hebrew)* Candelabrum

Mercedes *(Latin)* Reward

Mercy *(Middle English)* Compassion

Meredith *(Irish)* Protector from the sea

Mereki *(Australian Aboriginal)* Peace-maker

Merinda *(Australian Aboriginal)* Beautiful woman

Merle *(Latin)* Blackbird

Meryl See Merle

Messina *(Latin)* Middle child

Meta See Margaret

Mia *(Italian)* Mine

Michaela *(Hebrew)* Likeness to God

Michaelina See Michaela

Michaeline See Michaela

Michaella *(Italian)*

Michaela

Michelle *(Hebrew)* Who is like the Lord? *Feminine of* Michael

Michiko *(Japanese)* Righteous

Mignon *(French)* Delicate

Miguelita *(Spanish)* Michaela

Mikaela *See* Michaela

Milada *(Czech)* My love

Mildred *(Old English)* Kind counsellor

Millemurro *(Australian Aboriginal)* Pelican

Millicent *See* Melissa

Millie *See* Millicent/ Camille

Milly *See* Camille

Mimi *(French)* Miriam

Mina *See* Wilhelmina

Mindy *See* Wilhelmina

Minerva *(Greek)* Wisdom

Minette *(French)*

Minerva

Minkie *(Australian Aboriginal)* Daylight

Minna *(Old German)* Tender affection

Minta *(Greek)* Mint plant

Mintha *See* Minta

Mira *See* Myra

Mirabel *(Latin)* Beautiful

Mirabelle *(Spanish)* Mirabel

Miranda *(Latin)* Admirable

Mirelia *See* Myra

Mirelle *See* Myra

Miriam *(Hebrew)* Bitter

Mirilia *See* Myra

Mirna *See* Myrna

Missy *See* Melissa

Misty *(Old English)* Covered with mist

Mitzi *See* Miriam

Modesta *(Italian)* Modest one

Modestia *(Spanish)* Modest one

Modestine *(French)* Modest one

Modesty *(Latin)* Modest

Moibeal *(Scotch)* Mabel

Moibeal *(Scottish)* Mabel

Moina *See* Myrna

Moira *(Greek)* Fate

Mollie *(Irish)* Mary

Molly *See* Mollie

Mona *(Greek)* Alone

Monca *(Irish)* Monica

Monica *(Latin)* Advisor

Morag *(Gaelic)* Sun

Moreen *See* Maureen

Morgana *(Old Welsh)* Seashore

Moria *See* Maureen

Moriah *(Hebrew)* God is my teacher

Morna *(Gaelic)* Gentle

Moselle *(Hebrew)* Child rescued from the water

Moyna *See* Myrna

Muireall *(Scottish)* Muriel

Muirgheal *(Irish)* Muriel

Muriel *(Arabic)* Myrrh

Musetta *(Old French)* Pastoral song

Musidora *(Greek)* Gift of the Muses

Myfawny *(Welsh)* My precious one

Myra *(Latin)* Wonderful

Myrilla *See* Myra

Myrna *(Irish)* Polite

Myrtle *(Greek)* Myrtle tree

N

Naarah *(Hebrew)* Girl of our heart

Nadia *(French)* Hope

Nadine *(Slavic)* Nadia. *Feminine of* Nathan

Nairne *(Scottish)* From the river with alder trees

Nalani *(Hawaiian)*

Calmness of the heavens

Nan *See* Ann

Nance *See* Ann

Nancy *See* Ann

Nandalie *(Australian Aboriginal)* Fire

Nanette *(French)* Ann

Nani *(Hawaiian)* Beautiful

Naomi *(Hebrew)* Pleasant

Napea *(Latin)* Woman of the valleys

Nara *(Irish)* Happy

Narda *(Latin)* Perfume

Nardoo *(Australian Aboriginal)* Clover

Narelle *See* Helen

Nari *(Japanese)* Thunderbolt

Nastasha *(Russian)* Natalie

Nastassu *See* Natalie

Nasya *(Hebrew)* Miracle of God

Nata *(Hindustani)* Rope

dancer

Natala *See* Natalie

Natalia *(Spanish)* Natalie

Natalie *(Latin)* Nativity/Born on Christmas day. *Feminine of* Noel

Nataline *See* Natalie

Natasha *(Russian)* Natalie

Nathania *(Hebrew)* A gift from God

Natividad *(Spanish)* Christmas child

Neda *(Slavic)* Sunday's child. *Feminine of* Edward

Nelda *(Old English)* From a home at the elder-tree

Nelia *See* Cornelia

Nellie *See* Cornelia

Nellwyn *(Old English)* Friend of Nell

Neola *(Greek)* Youthful

Neoma *(Greek)* The new moon

Nerida *(Australian Aboriginal)* Flower

Nerine *(Greek)* Sea nymph

Nerissa *(Greek)* One from the sea

Nessa *(Norse)* Headland. *Also familiar of* Agnes

Netta *See* Antoinette

Nettie *See* Antoinette/Natalie

Neva *(Spanish)* White

Nevada *(Spanish)* White as snow

Ngoc Nhan *(Vietnamese)* Beautiful girl

Ngoc *(Vietnamese)* A gem

Nichole *See* Nicola

Nicholle *See* Nicola

Nicola *(Greek)* People's victory. *Feminine of* Nicholas

Nicole *See* Nicola

Nicolette *See* Nicola

Nike *(Greek)* Victory

Nikki *See* Nicola

Nina *(Spanish)* Girl

Ninette *See* Nina

Nissa *(Scandinavian)* Friendly elf

Nita *(American Indian)* Bear. *Also (Spanish)* Ann

Noel *(Latin)* Christmas child

Noelani *(Hawaiian)* Beautiful/Heavenly

Nola *(Latin)* Small bell. *Also (Irish)* Olivia

Nolana *See* Nola

Nona *(Latin)* Ninth child

Nora *See* Eleanor

Noreen *See* Honora

Norma *(Latin)* A rule/Pattern

Nova *(Latin)* New

Novia *(Spanish)* Sweetheart

Nu *(Vietnamese)* Woman

Nuala *(Irish)* Fair-shouldered

Nunkeri *(Australian*

Aboriginal) Excellent

Nydia *(Latin)* From the nest

Nyssa *(Greek)* Beginning

O

Obelia *(Greek)* A pointed pillar

Octavia *(Latin)* Eighth (child). *Feminine of* Octavius

Odele *See* Odelia

Odelia *(Greek)* Song

Odette *(French)* Home-lover

Ola *(Nordic)* Daughter

Olena *(Russian)* Light

Olethea *(Latin)* Truth

Olga *(Old Norse)* Holy one

Olien *(Russian)* Deer

Olinda *(Latin)* Fragrant

Olive *See* Olivia

Olivette *See* Olivia

Olivia *(Latin)* Olive tree

Olympia *(Greek)* Heavenly

Oma *(Arabic)* Commander. *Feminine of* Omar

Omega *(Greek)* Last-born

Ona *(Latin)* Unity

Ondine *(Latin)* Wave

Ooyelia *(Australian Aboriginal)* Compassionate

Opal *(Hindu)* Gemstone

Ophelia *(Greek)* Serpent/Wise

Ora *(Latin)* Golden

Oralee *(Hebrew)* Light

Oralia *See* Aurelia/Ora

Orelia *See* Aurelia

Oriana *(Latin)* Golden dawn

Oriel *(Latin)* Golden

Oriole *(Latin)* Fairhaired

Orsola *(Italian)* Ursula

Orsola *(Italian)* Ursula

Ortensia *(Italian)*
Hortense

Osanna *(Latin)*
Merciful one

Owena *(Welsh)*
Well-born

Ozora *(Hebrew)* Strength
of the Lord

P

Page *See* Paige

Paige *(Old English)*
Child

Palila *(Polynesian)* Bird

Pallas *(Greek)* Wisdom

Palma *(Latin)* Palm tree

Palmira *See* Palma

Palmyra *See* Palma

Paloma *(Spanish)* Dove

Palomita *See* Paloma

Pam *See* Pamela

Pamela *(Greek)*
Honey-sweet

Pammy *See* Pamela

Pandora *(Greek)* Gifted

Panphila *(Greek)* One
who loves

Pansy *(Greek)* Fragrant
as a flower

Panthea *(Greek)* Of all
the gods

Paola *(Italian)* Paula

Parnel *(Latin)* Rock

Parnella *(Old French)*
Little rock

Parthenia *(Greek)* Virgin

Paschasia *(Greek)*
Born at Easter

Pat *See* Patricia

Patience *(Latin)* Patient

Patrice *See* Patricia

Patricia *(Latin)*
Noble/Well-born

Patrizia *(Italian)* Patricia

Patsy *See* Patricia

Patti *See* Patricia

Patty *See* Patricia

Patya *(Australian
Aboriginal)* Flower

Paula *(Latin)* Small.

Feminine of Paul

Paulette *See* Paula

Paulina *(Spanish)* Paula

Pauline *See* Paula

Pavla *(Czech)* Paula

Pazia *(Hebrew)* Golden

Pearl *(Latin)* Pearl

Peggy *See* Margaret

Pelagia *(Greek)* The sea

Penelope *(Greek)* Weaver

Pennie *See* Penelope

Penny *See* Penelope

Penthea *(Greek)* Fifth child

Peony *(Greek)* Flower

Pepita *(Spanish)* Josephine

Perdita *(Latin)* Lost one

Perilla *(Latin-Greek)* A stone

Perlita *(Italian)* Pearl

Perrine *(French)* Petra

Persephone *(Greek)* Awe-inspiring

Persis *(Latin)* Persian

Peta *See* Petra

Petica *(Latin)* Noble one

Petra *(Greek)* A rock

Petrina *(Greek)* Steadfast as a rock

Petronelia *See* Petra

Petronia *See* Petra

Petronilla *See* Petra

Petronille *(German)* Petra

Petula *(Latin)* Seeker

Petunia *(Latin)* The flower

Phedra *(Greek)* Bright one

Philana *(Greek)* Loving

Philantha *(Greek)* One who loves flowers

Philippa *(Greek)* One who loves horses. *Feminine of* Philip

Phillida *(Greek)* Loving woman

Philomena *(Greek)* Lover of the moon

Phoebe *(Greek)* One who shines

Phoenix *(Greek)* Purple

Photina *(Greek)* Light

Phyllis *(Greek)* Green branch

Pia *(Italian)* Devout

Pierette *(French)* Little steadfast one. *Feminine of* Pierre

Pietra *(Italian)* Petra

Pilar *(Spanish)* A pillar

Pinterry *(Australian Aboriginal)* Star

Pipipa *(Australian Aboriginal)* Sandpiper

Pippa *See* Philippa

Placida *(Latin)* Gentle/Peaceful

Platona *(Greek)* Broad-shouldered. *Feminine of* Plato.

Polly *See* Paula

Pollyanna Polly+Anne

Polonia *(Latin)* Polish person

Pomona *(Latin)* Fruitful

Poppy *(Latin)* The flower

Portia *(Latin)* Offering

Prima *(Latin)* Firstborn

Primavera *(Latin)* New life/Springtime

Primrose *(Latin)* First rose

Priscilla *(Latin)* From long ago/Of ancient lineage

Prospera *(Latin)* Favourable

Pru *See* Prudence

Prudence *(Latin)* Discretion/Foresight

Prue *See* Prudence

Prunella *(Latin)* Plumcoloured

Psyche *(Greek)* Soul

Pyrena *(Greek)* Fruit kernel

Pythia *(Greek)* Prophet

Q

Quarralia *(Australian Aboriginal)* Star

Queena *(Old German)* Queen

Queenie *See* Queena

Quella *(Old English)* To pacify

Quenby *(Norse)* Wife

Querida *(Spanish)* Beloved

Quinta *(Latin)* Fifth (child). *Feminine of* Quintin

R

Raama *(Hebrew)* One who trembles

Rabia *(Arabic)* Spring

Rachael *See* Rachel

Rachel *(Hebrew)* An ewe/Innocent one

Rachele *(Italian)* Rachel

Rachelle *(French)* Rachel

Radella *(Old English)* Elf counsellor

Radinka *(Slavic)* Active

Radmilla *(Slavic)* One who works for the nation

Rae *(Old English)* Doe

Rafaella *(Italian)* Raphaela

Rahel *(German)* Rachel

Raina *(Old German)* Powerful

Raine *(Latin)* Dominance

Raisa *(French)* Trusting

Ramona *(Spanish)* Powerful

Rani *(Sanskrit)* Queen

Rania *See* Raisa

Ranita *(Hebrew)* Song

Raoghnailt *(Scottish)* Rachel

Raphaela *(Hebrew)*

Blessed healer. *Feminine of* Raphael

Raquel *(Spanish)* Rachel

Rasia *See* Rose

Raven *(Old English)* Black bird

Ray *See* Rachel

Reba *See* Rebecca

Rebecca *(Hebrew)* Bound (with rope)

Rebeka *See* Rebecca

Rebekah *See* Rebecca

Rechaba *(Hebrew)* Horsewoman

Regina *(Latin)* Queen

Reiko *(Japanese)* Gratitude

Reina *(Spanish)* Regina

Reine *(French)* Regina

Rena *(Hebrew)* Song

Renata *(Latin)* Born again

Renate *(German)* Renata

Renée *(French)* Renata

Renita *(Latin)* One who resists

Rewuri *(Australian Aboriginal)* Spring

Rexana *(Latin)* Regal

Rhea *(Greek)* Mother

Rhedyn *(Welsh)* Fern

Rheta *(Greek)* Orator

Rhiamon *(Welsh)* Witch

Rhiannon *(Welsh)* Nymph

Rhoda *(Greek)* Rose

Rhodeia *(Greek)* Rosy-cheeked

Rhodia *See* Rose

Rhonda *(Irish)* Strongly flowing river. *Also (Welsh)* Grand

Rhonwen *(Welsh)* Rowena

Ria *(Spanish)* River

Ricadonna *(Italian)* Ruling lady

Ricarda *(Old English)* Powerful ruler. *Feminine of* Richard

Rilla *(German)* Stream

Rillette *See* Rilla

Rina *See* Regina

Rinah *(Hebrew)* Song

Rioghnach *(Irish)* Regina

Risa *(Latin)* Laughter

Rita *(Greek)* Pearl

Riva *(French)* Shore

Roanna Rose+Anne

Roberta *(Old English)* Famous

Robin *See* Roberta

Robine *(French) See* Roberta

Robyn *See* Roberta

Rochelia *See* Rochelle

Rochelle *(French)* From the little rock

Rochette *See* Rochelle

Roderica *(Old German)* Famous ruler

Rohana *(Hindu)* Sandalwood

Rois *(Irish)* Rose

Rolanda *(Old German)* Famous. *Feminine of* Roland

Roma *(Latin)* Eternal city

Romaine *See* Roma

Romana *(Latin)* Woman of Rome

Romelle *See* Roma

Romula *(Latin)* Roman

Rona *(Scandinavian)* Mighty power. *Feminine of* Ronald

Ronalda *(Old German)* Powerful

Ronnie *See* Veronica

Rosa *(Italian)* Rose

Rosabel *(Latin)* Beautiful rose

Rosalie *(Latin)* Multitude of roses

Rosalind *(Greek)* Beautiful rose

Rosalynd *See* Rosalind

Rosamond *(Old German)* Famous guardian

Rosanna *(Latin)* Gracious rose

Rose *(Greek)* A rose

Roselani *(Polynesian)*

Roselle *See* Rose

Rosemary *(Latin)* Dew from the sea/The herb rose-mary

Rosetta *See* Rose

Roslyn *See* Rosalind

Rowena *(Old English)* Famous friend

Roxanna *(English)* Graceful rose. *Also (Persian)* Brilliant dawn

Roxanne *See* Roxanna

Roxine *See* Roxanna

Rozelia *See* Rose

Ruby *(Latin)* Red gemstone

Rufina *(Latin)* Red-haired

Ruth *(Hebrew)* Beautiful and compassionate

S

Saba *(Hebrew)* Old

Sabina *(Latin)* Woman of Sabine

Sabine *See* Sabina

Sabra *(Hebrew)* Thorny cactus. *Also* native-born Israeli

Sabrina *(Latin)* Princess

Sacha *(Greek)* Helper

Sacharissa *(Greek)* Sweet

Sachi *(Japanese)* Joy

Sadelia *See* Sarah

Sadhbba *(Irish)* Sophia

Sadie *See* Sarah

Sadira *(Persian)* Lotus tree

Saffron *(Arabic)* Yellow

Salaidh *(Scottish)* Sarah

Salena *(Latin)* Salty

Sallie *See* Sarah

Sally *See* Sarah

Salome *(Hebrew)* Peace

Salomi *See* Salome

Salvia *(Latin)* Sage

Salvina *See* Salvia

Samantha *(Aramaic)* Listener

Samara *(Hebrew)* Guarded (by God)

Samella *See* Samuela

Samuela *(Hebrew)* Name of God. *Feminine of* Samuel

Sancha *(Spanish)* Holy

Sancia *(Latin)* Sacred

Sandi *See* Alexandra

Sandi *See* Sandra

Sandie *See* Alexandra

Sandra *(Greek)* Protector. *Also short for* Alexandra, Cassandra

Sandra *See* Alexandra

Sandy *See* Alexandra

Sanura *(Swahili)* Kitten-like

Sapphira *(Greek)* Sapphire gem

Sara *See* Sarah

Sarah *(Hebrew)* Princess

Sarene *See* Sarah

Sarette *See* Sarah

Sari *See* Sarah

Sarie *See* Sarah

Sarine *See* Sarah

Sarka *(Czech) See* Sarah

Saschal *See* Sasha

Sasha *(Russian) short for* Alexandra

Sashenka *See* Sasha

Savanna *(Spanish)* An open plain

Savannah *See* Savanna

Savina *See* Sabina.

Saxona *(Old English)* A Saxon

Scarlett *(Middle English)* Scarlet colour

Schyler *See* Skye

Sebastiane *(Latin)* August person. *Feminine of* Sebastian

Sebastians *See*

Sebastiane

Secunda *(Latin)* Second child

Seirian *(Welsh)* Sparkling/Bright

Sela *See* Selene

Selene *(Greek)* The moon

Selia *See* Selene

Selie *See* Selene

Selima *(Hebrew)* Peaceful. *Feminine of* Solomon

Selma *(Irish)* Fair. *Feminine of* Anselm

Semira *(Hebrew)* As tall as the heavens

Sena *See* Selene

Seonaid *(Scottish)* Jane

Septima *(Latin)* Seventh child

Serafina *See* Seraphina

Seraphina *(Hebrew)* Devout

Serena *(Latin)* Tranquil

Serilda *(Old German)* Armour-clad battlemaid

Serita *(Italian)* Sarah

Shaina *(Hebrew)* Beautiful

Shana *See* Shauna

Shannon *(Irish)* Slow stream

Sharicen *See* Caroline

Shariene *See* Caroline

Sharleen *See* Caroline

Sharline *See* Caroline

Sharon *(Hebrew)* Beautiful princess

Shauna *(Irish)* Jane

Shawna *See* Shauna

Sheba *See* Saba

Sheena *(Irish)* God is gracious

Sheha *(Irish)* Sabina

Sheila *(Irish)* Cecilia

Sheina *(Hebrew)* Gift from God

Shelby *(Old English)* From the estate

Shelley *See* Rochelle

Sher *(Old English)* Shrine

Sheree *See* Charlotte

Sheryl *See* Shirley

Shiela *See* Sheila

Shifra *(Hebrew)* Beautiful

Shina *(Japanese)* Virtue

Shiri *(Hebrew)* My song

Shiriene *See* Shirley

Shirley *(Old English)* Bright meadow

Shoshana *See* Susan

Shulamith *(Hebrew)* Peace

Sibeal *(Irish)* Sibyl

Sibena *(Greek)* A mermaid siren who sings sweetly

Sibille *See* Sibyl

Sibley *(Old English)* Sibling

Sibyl *(Greek)* Prophetess

Sibylla *(Dutch)* Sibyl

Sidba *(Latin)* Glittering/Starlike

Sidney *See* Sydney

Sidonia *See* Sydney

Sigfreda *(Old German)* Victorious but peaceful. *Feminine of* Siegfried

Signa *(Latin)* One who signs

Signe *See* Signa

Sigrid *(Norse)* Great victory

Silva *See* Sylvia

Silvia *See* Sylvia

Simone *(Hebrew)* God has heard

Simonette *(French)* Simone

Siobhán *(Hebrew)* One who is admired

Sirena *(Greek)* Temptress

Sirri *(Finnish)* Sarah

Skye *(Dutch)* One who shelters

Skyla *See* Skye

Skylar *See* Skye

Solana *(Spanish)* Sunshine

Solvig *(Old German)* Victorious battlemaid

Sonia *See* Sophia

Sonja *See* Sophia

Sonya *See* Sophia

Sophia *(Greek)* Wisdom

Sophie *See* Sophia

Sophronia *(Greek)* Sensible one

Sorcha *(Celtic)* Bright person. *Also (Irish)* Sarah

Sosanna *(Irish)* Susan

Stacey *See* Anastasia

Stacia *See* Anastasia

Stacie *See* Anastasia

Stella *(Latin)* Star. *Also short for* Estelle

Stephanie *(Greek)* Crowned. *Feminine of* Stephen

Stockard *(Old English)* Tough tree stump

Sue *Short for* Susan

Sula *(Icelandic)* Large sea bird

Sunny *See* Sophia

Susan *(Hebrew)* Lily

Susannah *See* Susan

Susanne *See* Susan

Suzanne *See* Susan

Suzette *See* Susan

Sybil *See* Sibyl

Sydel *(Hebrew)* Enchantress

Sydney *(Old French)* From the city of St Denis

Sylgwyn *(Welsh)* Born on Whitsunday

Sylvia *(Latin)* From the forest

Syna *(Greek)* Together

T

Tabina *(Arabic)* Muhammed's follower

Tabitha *(Aramaic)* Gazelle

Tacita *(Latin)* Silent

Taffy *(Welsh)* Beloved

Taima *(North American Indian)* Crash of thunder

Talia *(Greek)* Blooming

Talitha *(Aramaic)* Maiden

Tallulah *(American Indian)* Fast-flowing water

Tama *(Hebrew)* Astonishment

Tamar *See* Tamara

Tamara *(Hebrew)* Palm tree

Tamarind *(Arabic)* Indian date

Tami *(Japanese)* People

Tamika *(Japanese)* People

Tammy *(Hebrew)* Perfection

Tamsin *See* Thomasina

Tania *(Russian)* Fairy queen

Tanya *See* Tania

Tara *(Irish)* Rocky pinnacle

Taryn *See* Tara

Tasha *See* Natasha

Tasia *See* Anastasia

Tatum *(Old English)* Cheerful

Teena *See* Christina

Tempest *(Old French)* Stormy person

Teodora *(Italian)* Theodora

Terentia *(Greek)* Guardian

Teresa *See* Theresa

Terese *See* Theresa

Teresita *See* Theresa

Teressa *See* Theresa

Terrie *See* Theresa

Terry *See* Theresa

Tertia *(Latin)* The third

Tess *See* Tessa

Tessa *(Greek)* The fourth

Thaddea *(Greek)* Courageous. *Feminine of* Thaddeus

Thalia *(Greek)* Joyful/Flourishing

Thea *(Greek)* Goddess

Theano *(Greek)* Divine name

Thecla *(Greek)* Divinely famous

Thelma *(Greek)* Nursling

Theodora *(Greek)* Divine gift

Theodosia *See* Theodora

Theola *(Greek)* From heaven

Theone *(Greek)* In God's name

Theophania *(Greek)* Appearance of God

Theophila *(Greek)* Beloved of God

Theora *(Greek)* One who contemplates

Thera *(Greek)* Untamed

Theresa *(Greek)* Reaper

Thetis *(Greek)* Determined

Thiewie *(Australian Aboriginal)* Flower

Thirsa *(Hebrew)* Pleasant

Thomasina *(Hebrew)* Twin. *Feminine of* Thomas

Thora *(Norse)* Thunderer. *Feminine of* Thor

Thyra *(Greek)* Shield-bearer

Tia *(Egyptian)* Princess

Tibbie *See* Tiberia

Tibby *See* Tiberia

Tibelda *(Old German)* Boldest of the tribe

Tiberia *(Latin)* From the river Tiber

Tierney *(Irish Gaelic)* Grandchild of the lordly

Tiffani *See* Tiffany

Tiffanie *See* Tiffany

Tiffany *(French)* God's manifestation

Tikvah *(Hebrew)* Hope

Tilda *See* Matilda

Tilpulun *(Australian Aboriginal)* Sparkling

Timmy *See* Timothea

Timothea *(Greek)* To honour God. *Feminine of* Timothy

Tina *See* Christina

Ting *(Chinese)* Graceful

Tiphanie *See* Tiffany

Tirza *(Hebrew)* Cypress tree

Titania *(Greek)* Giant

Tobey *(Hebrew)* God is good. *Feminine of* Tobias

Toinette *See* Antoinette

Toireasa *(Irish)* Theresa

Toni *See* Antonia/ Antoinette

Tonia *See* Antoinette

Tonie *See* Antoinette

Tonya *See* Antoinette

Topaz *(Latin)* Topaz gemstone

Tracey *See* Tracy/ Theresa

Tracy *(Irish)* One who battles

Traviata *(Italian)* One who goes astray

Tricia *See* Patricia

Trina *See* Katherine

Trinity *(Latin)* Threefold

Trish *See* Patricia

Trisha *See* Patricia

Trista *(Latin)* Melancholy. *Feminine of* Tristan

Trixie *See* Beatrice

Trixy *See* Beatrice

Trudie *See* Trudy. *Also short for* Gertrude

Trudy *(Old German)* Beloved. *Also short for* Gertrude

Tullia *(Irish)* Quiet one.

Turquoise *(French)* Turkish stone

Twyla *(Middle English)* Woven of double thread

Tzigane *(Hungarian)* Gypsy

U

Uda *(Old German)*
Prosperous

Udelle *See* Uda

Ula *(Irish)* Sea jewel

Ulima *(Arabic)*
Wise/Learned

Ulrica *(Old German)*
Ruler of all. *Feminine of*
Ulric

Ultima *(Latin)* Final

Ulva *(Old English)* Wolf

Umeko *(Japanese)*
Plum-blossom child

Una *(Latin)* Number one

Undine *(Latin)* Wave

Unity *(Middle English)*
United

Unnea *(Old Norse)*
Linden-tree

Urania *(Greek)* Heavenly

Ursola *See* Ursula

Ursula *(Latin)* Little bear

Ursule *(French)* Ursula

Ursuline *See* Ursula

Uta *(Old German)*
Heroine

V

Val *See* Valerie

Vala *(Gothic)* Chosen one

Valborga *(Old German)*
Protecting ruler

Valda *(Old Norse)* Ruler

Valentia *(Latin)* Strong

Valentine *See* Valentia

Valeria *See* Valerie

Valerie *(Old French)*
Strong

Valeska *(Slavic)*
Glorious ruler

Valma *(Welsh)*
Mayflower

Valonu *(Latin)* From the
vale

Vanessa *(Greek)*
Butterfly

Vania *(Hebrew)* God's gift

Vanora *(Scottish)* Genevieve

Varina *(Slavic)* Stranger

Varvara *(Slavic)* Barbara

Vashti *(Persian)* Beautiful

Veda *(Sanskrit)* Wise

Vedette *(Italian)* Guardian

Vega *(Arabic)* One who falls

Velda *(Old German)* Wise

Veliya *(Slavic)* One who is great

Velma *See* Wilhelmina

Velvet *(Latin)* Soft/Velvety

Ventura *(Spanish)* Good luck

Venus *(Latin)* Goddess of love

Vera *(Latin)* True. *Also short for* Veronica

Verda *(Latin)* Young/fresh

Verena *(Old German)* Defender

Veritie *See* Verity

Verity *(Latin)* Truth

Verna *(Latin)* Like a spring

Veronica *(Latin)* Truthful

Veronike *(German)* Veronica

Veronique *(French)* Veronica

Vespera *(Latin)* Evening

Vesta *(Latin)* Goddess of the home

Vevila *(Irish)* Melodious lady

Vicki *See* Victoria

Vickie *See* Victoria

Victoire *(French)* Victoria

Victoria *(Latin)* Victory. *Feminine of* Victor

Victorine *See* Victoria

Vida *(Hebrew)* Beloved. *Also feminine of* David

Vidonia *(Portuguese)* Vine branch

Vigilu *(Latin)* Vigilant

Vignette *(French)* Little vine

Villette *(French)* From the country estate

Vincentia *(Latin)* One who conquers. *Feminine of* Vincent

Vinita *See* Venus.

Viola *See* Violet

Violante *(Spanish)* Violet

Violet *(Latin)* Violet flower

Violetta *See* Violet

Violette *(French)* Violet

Virgelu *(Latin)* One who carries a staff

Virginia *(Latin)* Virginal/Pure

Virginie *(French)* Virginia

Viridis *(Latin)* Freshly blooming

Vita *(Latin)* Life

Vitoria *See* Victoria

Vivian *(Latin)* Full of life

Viviana *(Italian)* Vivian

Vivienne *(French)* Vivian

Volante *(Italian)* One who flies

Voleta *(Old French)* A flowing veil

Vonny *See* Veronica

W

Walda *(Old German)* Warrior

Walker *(Old English)* Thickener of cloth

Wallis *(Old English)* From Wales

Wambalano *(Australian Aboriginal)* Beautiful

Waminda *(Australian Aboriginal)* Friend

Wanda *(Old German)* Wanderer

Wanetta *(Old English)* Pale one

Warda *(Old German)* Guardian. *Feminine of* Ward

Warrah *(Australian Aboriginal)* Honeysuckle

Warranunna *(Australian Aboriginal)* A bee

Wendy *See* Gwendolyn

Wenona *(American Indian)* First-born

Weringerong *(Australian Aboriginal)* Lyre bird

Wesley *(Old English)* From the western meadow

Whitney *(Old English)* From the white island

Wilda *(Old English)* Willow

Wilfreda *(Old German)* Peacemaker

Wilhelmina *(Old German)* Determined protector. *Feminine of* William

Willow *(English)* Willow tree

Wilma *See* Wilhelmina

Wilona *(Old English)* Desired

Wilva *(Old German)* Determined

Winema *(American Indian)* Female chief

Winifred *(Old German)* Peaceful friend

Winona *(American Indian)* Friend/First-born

Winsome *(English)* Pleasant/Good-looking

Wirreecoo *(Australian Aboriginal)* Tea-tree

Woorak *(Australian Aboriginal)* Honeysuckle

Wren *(Old English)* The bird

Wynne *(Irish)* Fair/white. *Also short for* Gwendolyn

X, Y, Z

Xanthe *(Greek)* Golden

Xaviera *(Arabic)* Brilliant

Xena *(Greek)* Hospitable

Xylia *(Greek)* From the woods

Xylophila *(Greek)* Lover of the woods

Yasmin *See* Jasmin

Yasu *(Japanese)* Tranquil one

Yedda *(Old English)* Singer

Yesima *(Hebrew)* Strength

Yetta *(Old English)* One who gives

Ynez *(Spanish)* Agnes

Yoko *(Japanese)* Positive

Yolanda *See* Yolande

Yolande *(Greek)* Violet (the flower)

Yvonne *(French)* Archer

Zabrina *(Old English)* Royal

Zada *(Syrian)* Lucky

Zahara *(African)* Flower

Zaida *See* Zada

Zandra *See* Alexandra

Zandra *See* Alexandra

Zaneta *See* Jane

Zara *(Hebrew)* Dawn/Prosperous

Zea *(Latin)* Kind of grain

Zelia *(Greek)* Zealous

Zelma *See* Selma

Zena *(Greek)* Hospitable

Zenda *(Persian)* Womanly

Zenia *See* Xena

Zenia *See* Zenobia

Zenobia *(Greek)* Given life (by the God Zeus)

Zephaniah *(Hebrew)* Whom the Lord has hidden

Zephirah *(Hebrew)* Dawn

Zephyr *(Greek)* Wind

Zerelda *(Old German)*
Armoured woman
warrior

Zerlina *(Old German)*
Serene

Zerlinda *(Hebrew)*
Delightful dawn

Zetta *(Hebrew)* Olive

Zeva *(Hebrew)* Wolf

Zilla *(Hebrew)*
Shadow/Shade

Zina *(Hebrew)*
Abundance

Zinnia *(Latin)* Name of a
flower

Zippora *(Hebrew)*
Beauty

Zita *(Irish)* Enticing

Zoe *(Greek)* Life

Zofia *(Polish)* Sophia

Zola *(Italian)* Ball or
mound of earth

Zona *(Latin)* Girdle

Zora *(Slavic)*
Dawn/Aurora

Zosima *(Greek)* Wealthy
woman

Zsa Zsa *(Hungarian)*
Susan

Zuleika *(Persian)*
Brilliant beauty

g i r l s

Names
for
BOYS

A

Aaron *(Hebrew)*
Enlightened/Exalted

Abad *(Spanish)* Abbot

Abadi *(Arabic)* Eternal

Abba *See* Abbot

Abbas *(Arabic)* Uncle of
Muhammed

Abbe *(French)* Abbot

Abboid *(Gaelic)* Abbot

Abbot *(Anglo-Saxon)*
Father (of the abbey)

Abdul *(Arabic)* Son
of/Allah's servant

Abel *(Hebrew)* Breath

Abelard *(Old German)*
Noble/Ambitious

Abner *(Hebrew)* Divine
father

Abod *See* Abbot

Abott *(French)* Abbot

Abraham *(Hebrew)*
Father of the multitude

Abrahin *(Spanish)*
Abraham

Abramo *(Italian)*
Abraham

Absalom *(Hebrew)*
Father of peace

Abu-Sharif *(Arabic)*
Father of Sharif

Achad Ha'am *(Arabic)*
One of the people

Achilles *(Greek)*
Without lips

Acton *(Irish)* Village
with oak trees

Adair *(Irish)* From the
oak tree ford

Adam *(Hebrew)* Man of
the red earth

Adamo *(Italian)* Adam

Adamson *(Hebrew)*
Adam's son

Adan *(Spanish)* Adam

Adas *(Portuguese)* Adam

Addison *(Old English)*
Adam's son

Adel *(Teutonic)* Noble

Adelbert *See* Albert

Adelhard (*German*) Nobly resolute

Adhamh (*Irish, Scottish*) Adam

Adilo (*German*) Noble

Adin (*Hebrew*) Sensual

Adlai (*Hebrew*) My witness

Adler (*Old German*) Eagle

Adley (*Hebrew*) The fairminded

Adney (*Old English*) Dweller on the island of a nobleman

Adoffo (*Spanish, Italian*) Adolph

Adolf *See* Adolph

Adolfo (*Spanish*) Adolph

Adolph (*Old German*) Noble wolf/Hero

Adolphs (*French*) Adolph

Adolphu (*Swedish*) Adolph

Adon (*Hebrew*) Lord

Adoni (*Australian Aboriginal*) Sunset

Adonis (*Greek*) Handsome

Adrian (*Latin*) Dark one

Adriano (*Italian*) Adrian

Adriel (*Hebrew*) God's Kingdom

Aeneas (*Greek*) Praised one

Agamemnon (*Greek*) Resolute

Agatho (*Greek*) Good

Agilio (*Latin*) Agile

Agostino (*Italian*) Anguish

Ahab (*Hebrew*) Uncle

Ahearn (*Celtic*) Lord of the horses

Ahearn *See* Ahearn

Aherin *See* Ahearn

Aherne *See* Ahearn

Ahmad (*Arabic*) Comforter

Ahmed (*Arabic*) Most highly paid

Ahrens (*German*) Eagle power

Ahzab *(Arabic)* Confederate

Aidan *(Irish)* Small fiery one

Aidwin *See* Alden

Aikane *(Polynesian)* Friendly

Aiken *(Old English)* Made of oak

Ailbert *(Scottish)* Albert

Ailean *(Scottish)* Alan

Ailfrid *(Irish)* Alfred

Ailin *(Irish)* Alan

Aindreas *(Gaelic)* Andrew

Ainsley *See* Ainslie

Ainslie *(Old English)* Of the meadow

Airik *(Swedish)* Alarik

Ajax *(Greek)* Eagle

Akbar *(Arabic)* Name of a great Mogul Emperor

Akelina *(Russian)* Eagle

Akil *(Arabic)* Intelligent

Akiyama *(Japanese)* Autumn

Aksel *(German)* Tiny oak tree

Alabhaois *(Irish) See* Louis

Aladdin *(Arabic)* Servant of Allah

Alain *(French)* Alan

Alair *(Irish)* Cheerful

Alaister *See* Alexander

Alan *(Irish)* Handsome

Alano *(Italian)* Alan

Alard *(French)* Allard

Alaric *(Old German)* Supreme ruler

Alarico *(Spanish)* Alarik

Alasdair *See* Alexander

Alawn *(Welsh)* Harmony

Alba *(Australian Aboriginal)* Wind

Alban *(Irish)* Alben

Alben *(Latin)* Fair-complexioned

Alberik *(Swedish)* Aubrey

Albert *(Old German)* Noble/Bright/Industrious

Albertino *(Italian)* Albert

Alberto *(Italian, Spanish)* Albert

Albie *See* Albert

Albin *See* Alben

Albrecht *See* Albert

Alcott *(Old English)* From the old cottage

Alden *(Old English)* Old and wise protector/Friend

Alder *(Old English)* Alder tree

Aldin *See* Alden

Aldis *See* Aldous

Aldo *(Old German)* Old and wise

Aldous *(Old German)* Old and wise

Aldric *See* Aldrich

Aldrich *(Old English)* Old and wise ruler

Aldridge *(Old English)* Dairy farm in the alders

Aldwin *(Old English)* Old friend

Aldwyn *See* Alden

Aleik *(Russian)* Alexander

Alejandro *(Spanish)* Alexander

Aleksandr *(Russian)* Alexander

Alessandro *(Italian)* Alexander

Alexander *(Greek)* Defender/Helper of mankind

Alexandrè *(French)* Alexander

Alexio *(Portuguese)* Alexander

Alexis *(Greek)* Defender

Alfonso *See* Alphonso

Alford *(Old English)* From the old ford

Alfred *(Old English)* Wise/Elf counselor

Alfredo *(Italian)* Alfred

Alger *(Old German)* Noble spearman. *Short for* Algernon

Algernon *(Old French)* Bearded

Ali *(Arabic)* Exalted/Greatest

Alik *See* Alexander

Alistair *See* Alexander

Alister *See* Alexander

Allan *See* Alan

Allard *(Old English)* Brave/Noble

Allen *See* Alan

Allister *See* Alexander

Allyn *See* Alan

Almo *(Old English)* Noble and famous

Aloin *See* Aluin

Alois *(Hungarian)* Aloysius

Alonzo *(Spanish)* Alphonse

Aloys *See* Aloysius

Aloysius *(Latin)* Famous warrior

Alpheus *(Greek)* River god

Alphonse *(Old German)* Noble/Prepared

Alphonso *(German)* Noble and prepared

Alpin *(Scottish)* Blond

Alric *(Old German)* All powerful

Alroy *(Irish)* Red-haired young man

Alsandair *(Irish)* Alexander

Alston *(Old English)* Nobleman's estate

Altman *(Old German)* Wise old man

Alton *(Old English)* Inhabitant of the old town

Aluin *(French)* Alvin

Aluino *(Spanish)* Alvin

Alva *(Latin)* Blond

Alvah *(Hebrew)* Exalted

Alvin *(Old German)* Beloved by all

Alvis *(Old Norse)* All-wise

Alwin *(German)* Alvin

Alwyn *(Old English)* Old and noble friend

Amadeus *(Latin)* Beloved of God

Amahl *(Hebrew)* Labour

Amama *(Polynesian)* Open mouthed

Amandus *(Latin)* Worthy of love

Amaroo *(Australian Aboriginal)* Beautiful

Amasa *(Hebrew)* One who bears a burden

Amatziah *(Hebrew)* Strength of God

Ambler *(Old English)* Stablekeeper

Ambrogio *(Italian)* Ambrose

Ambroise *(French)* Ambrose

Ambros *(Irish)* Ambrose

Ambrose *(Greek)* Immortal

Ambrosio *(Spanish)* Ambrose

Ambrosius *(Dutch, German, Swedish)* Ambrose

Amerigo *(Italian)* Work

Amery *See* Amory

Amfrid *(German)* Ancestor peace

Amico *(Italian)* Friend

Amiel *(Hebrew)* Lord of my people

Amin *(Hebrew)* Trust

Amirov *(Hebrew)* My people are great

Ammon *(Egyptian)* Hidden

Amory *(Old German)* Famous and divine ruler

Amos *(Hebrew)* Burden

Amund *(Scandinavian)* Divine protection

Amyas *(Latin)* Love

An-Nur *(Arabic)* Light

Ananda *(Sanskrit)* To bless

Ananias *(Greek)* God's mercy

Anastasius *(Greek)*

Resurrection

Anatol *(Slavic)* Anatole

Anatole *(Greek)* Man from the east

Anatolio *(Spanish)* Anatole

Anbiorn *(Norse)* Eagle

Ancel *(Latin)* Servant

Anders *(Scandinavian)* Andrew

Andrè *(French)* Andrew

Andreas *(Dutch, German)* Andrew

Andrej *(Slavic)* Andrew

Andrew *(Greek)* Manly

Androcles *(Greek)* Man/Glory

Angelo *(Greek)* Angel

Angus *(Scottish)* Unique choice

Annan *(Celtic)* From the stream

Anno *(Hebrew)* Grace. *Also masculine of* Anne

Anntoin *(Irish)* Anthony

Ansel *(Old French)* Follower of a nobleman

Anselm *(Old German)* Divine soldier

Anselme *(French)* Anselm

Anselmi *(Italian)* Anselm

Anselmo *(Spanish, Portuguese)* Anselm

Ansheim *(German)* Anselm

Ansley *(Old English)* From the pasture meadow of the awe-inspiring one

Anson *(Old English)* Son of the awe-inspiring one

Anthony *(Latin)* Priceless

Antoine *(French)* Anthony

Anton *(German)* Anthony

Antonio *(Italian, Spanish, Portuguese)* Anthony

Anwell *(Welsh)* Dearest

111

Anyon *(Welsh)* Anvil

Aodh *(Irish)* Hugh

Aoidh *(Scottish)* Hugh

Apollo *(Greek)* Beautiful man

Aquila *(Latin)* Eagle

Arafat *(Arabic)* Mount of recognition

Araldo *(Italian)* Harold

Aralt *(Irish)* Harold

Araluen *(Australian Aboriginal)* Place of water lilies

Aram *(Hebrew)* Height

Archambault *(French)* Archibald

Archard *(French)* Sacred/Powerful

Archer *(Old English)* Bowman

Archibald *(Old German)* Noble/Bold

Archie *See* Archibald

Archimbald *(German)* Archibald

Archimedes *(Greek)* Master mind

Arden *(Latin)* Ardent

Ardley *(Old English)* From the meadow of the home-lover

Ardmore *(Latin)* More ardent

Arend *(Dutch)* Arnold

Argyle *(Gaelic)* Irishman

Ari *(Hebrew)* Lion

Aric *(Old English)* Holy ruler

Ariel *(Hebrew)* God's lion

Aries *(Latin)* A ram

Ariki *(Polynesian)* Chief

Aristotle *(Greek)* Name of famous philosopher

Arje *(Dutch)* Adrian

Arlen *(Irish)* Pledge

Armand *(French)* Herman

Armando *(Spanish)* Herman

Armstrong *(Old English)* Strong-armed warrior

Arnaldo *(Spanish)* Arnold

Arnaud *(French)* Arnold

Arne *(Old German)* Eagle

Arnold *(Old German)* Powerful as an eagle

Arnoldo *(Italian)* Arnold

Arnoux *(French)* Arne

Aron *See* Aaron

Artair *(Scottish)* Arthur

Arthur *(Celtic)* Strong/Noble

Artur *(German)* Arthur

Arturo *(Italian)* Arthur

Artus *(French)* Arthur

Arvad *(Hebrew)* Wanderer

Asa *(Hebrew)* Healer

Ascot *(Old English)* One who lives at the east cottage

Ashburn *(Old English)* Ash-tree brook

Ashburton *(Old English)* Ash tree

Ashby *(Scandinavian)* From the ash-tree farm

Asher *(Hebrew)* Lucky

Ashley *(Old English)* One who lives by the ash-tree meadow

Ashton *(Old English)* One who lives at the ash-tree farm

Asim *(Arabic)* Protector

Aston *(Old English)* Eastern place

Asvald *(Norse)* Divine strength

Atherton *(Old English)* One who lives at the farm with a spring

Athol *(Scottish)* Name of a place in Scotland

Auberon *(Old German)* King of the fairies

Aubin *(French)* Fair/Blond

Aubrey *(Old French)* Blond ruler

Audric *(French)* Aldrich

August *(Latin)* Royal dignity. *Also* the month

Aurelius *(Latin)* Golden

Austen *See* August

Austin *See* August

Avan *(Hebrew)* Proud

Averell *(Middle English)* Born in April

Avery *(Old English)* Elf-ruler

Axel *(Hebrew)* Trustworthy/Dependable

Aylward *(Old English)* Noble guardian

Aziz *(Arabic)* Mighty

B

Baiardo *(Italian)* Bayard

Bailey *(Old French)* Bailiff

Bailie *See* Bailey

Baillie *See* Bailey

Bainbridge *(Irish)* Fair bridge

Baird *(Irish)* Minstrel

Bais *(Arabic)* He who wakes

Baker *(Old English)* A baker

Bala-Rama *(Sanskrit)* Elder brother

Baldassare *(Italian)* Balthasar

Baldemar *(Old German)* Bold/Famous

Balder *(Old English)* Bold army leader

Baldwin *(Old German)* Bold friend

Balfour *(Scottish)* Pasture

Ballard *(Old German)* Bold/Strong

Baltasar *(German, Swedish)* Balthasar

Balthasar *(Greek)* May the Lord protect the king

Bancroft *(Old English)* Bean field

114

Bapp *(Australian Aboriginal)* Blue gum tree

Baptysta *(Polish)* Baptist

Baradine *(Australian Aboriginal)* Red wallaby

Barber *(Latin)* Beard

Barclay *(Old English)* From the meadow of birches

Barde *(French)* Barclay

Bardick *(Old English)* Ruler with an axe

Bardin *(Australian Aboriginal)* Ironbark tree

Bardo *(Australian Aboriginal)* Water

Bardolf *(Old English)* Big wolf

Baringa *(Australian Aboriginal)* A light

Barlow *(Old English)* Barren hill

Barnabas *(Greek)* Son of prophecy

Barnaby *See* Barnabas

Barnard *(French)* Bernard

Barnett *(Old English)* Nobleman

Barney *See* Bernard

Barnum *(Old English)* House of stone

Baron *(Old English)* Nobleman

Barr *(Old German)* Bear

Barret *(Old German)* Strong as a bear

Barrie *(Irish)* Spear

Barris *(Old Welsh)* Son of Harry

Barry *(Irish)* Spear

Bart *See* Bartholomew

Bartel *See* Bartholomew

Barthel *(German)* Bartholomew

Bartholomeus *(Dutch)* Bartholomew

Bartholomew *(Hebrew)* Son of the furrows

Bartley *(Old English)* Bart's meadow

Bartolome *(Spanish)*
Bartholomew

Bartolomeo *(Italian)*
Bartholomew

Barton *(Old English)*
Barley farm

Baruch *(Hebrew)*
Blessed

Barwon *(Australian Aboriginal)* Magpie

Basil *(Greek)* Majestic

Basilio *(Italian)* Basil

Basilius *(Dutch, German, Swedish)* Basil

Basir *(Turkish)*
Clever/Discerning

Baudier *(French)* Balder

Baum *(German)* Tree

Baumer *(French)*
Baldemar

Baxter *(Old English)*
Baker

Bayard *(Old English)*
Redbrown

Beacher *(Old English)*
One who lives by the beech tree

Beaman *(Old English)*
Beekeeper

Beamer *(Old English)*
Trumpeter

Bearnard *(Gaelic)*
Bernard

Beathan *(Scottish)*
Benjamin

Beattie *(Latin)* One who bestows blessings

Beau *(French)* Handsome

Beaufort *(Old French)*
From the beautiful fort

Beauregard *(Old French)* Handsome

Beauvais *(French)* Bevis

Beck *(Scandinavian)*
Brook

Bela *(French)* Handsome

Belden *(Old English)*
One who lives in the beautiful glen

Beldon *See* Belden

Bellamy *(Old French)*
Handsome friend

Belshazzar *(Hebrew)*
Balthasar

Ben *(Hebrew)* Son. *Also diminutive of* Benjamin

Benedetto *(Italian)* Benedict

Benedict *(Latin)* Blessed

Benedikt *(German, Swedish)* Benedict

Beniamino *(Italian)* Benjamin

Benito *(Italian)* Benedict

Benjamin *(Hebrew)* Son of the right hand.

Bennett *(French)* Little blessed one

Bennie *See* Benjamin

Benny *See* Benjamin

Benoit *(French)* Benedict

Benoni *(Hebrew)* Son of my sorrow

Benson *(Hebrew)* Son of Benjamin

Bentley *(Old English)* From the moor

Benton *(Old English)* From the farm with bent grass

Benvenuto *(Italian)* The right way

Beppi *(Italian)* Joseph

Beppo *See* Joseph

Berend *(German)* Bernard

Berenger *(Old German)* Bear spear

Beresford *(Old English)* From the barleyford

Berg *(German)* From the mountain

Bergen *(Old German)* Hill

Berger *(French)* Shepherd

Bergren *(Scandinavian)* Mountain stream

Berk *See* Burke

Berkeley *See* Barclay

Bern *(Old German)* Bear. *Also Short for* Bernard

Bernard *(Old German)* Brave as a bear

Bernardo *(Italian, Spanish)* Bernard

Berringar *(Australian Aboriginal)* Sunset

Bert *(Old English)*
Bright/Shining. *Short for* Albert, Herbert

Berthold *(Old German)*
Brilliant ruler

Berthoud *(French)*
Berthold

Bertold *See* Berthold

Bertoldi *(Italian)*
Berthold

Berton *(Old English)*
Fortified town

Bertram *(Old English)*
Brilliant raven

Bertrand *(French)*
Bertram

Bertrando *(Italian)*
Bertram

Berwick *(Old English)*
Barley farm

Bevan *(Welsh)* Son of a warrior

Beverly *(Old English)*
Beaver stream

Bevis *(Old French)* Fair view

Beynon *(Welsh)* Reliable

Bhaltair *(Scottish)* Walter

Bhima *(Sanskrit)*
Mighty one

Biagio *(Italian)* Blaze

Bighta *(Persian)* God's gift

Bill *See* William

Billy *See* William

Biloela *(Australian Aboriginal)* Cockatoo

Bilyana *(Australian Aboriginal)* Wedgetailed eagle

Bing *(Old German)*
Kettle-shaped hollow

Bingham *(Old English)*
One who lives by the bridge

Birch *(Old English)* Birch tree

Birney *(Old English)*
One who lives on the brook-island

Bjorn *(Scandinavian)* Bear

Blade *(Old English)*
Prosperous

Blaine *(Irish)* Lean

Blair *(Irish)* From the plain

Blaise *(French)* Blaze

Blake *(Old English)* Dark

Blakeley *(Old English)* From the black meadow

Blanco *(Spanish)* White

Bland *(Latin)* Gentle

Blanford *(Old English)* River crossing of the grey-haired one

Blas *(Spanish)* Blaze

Blasien *(German)* Blaze

Blasius *(Swedish)* Blaze

Blayne *See* Blaine

Bob *See* Robert

Bobby *See* Robert

Boden *(Old French)* Messenger

Bogart *(Old French)* Strong bow

Bogdan *(Slavonic)* God's gift

Bonar *(Old French)* Gentle

Bond *(Old English)* Tiller of the soil

Boniface *(Italian)* Handsome

Boone *(Old French)* Good

Booth *(Middle English)* One who lives in a hut

Borg *(Scandinavian)* From the castle

Boris *(Russian)* Warrior

Boswell *(Old French)* Settlement in the forest

Bosworth *(Old English)* Boar enclosure

Bourke *See* Burke

Bourn *See* Burne

Bourne *(Old English)* From the brook

Bowie *(Irish)* Yellow-haired

Boyce *(Old French)* From the wood

Boyd *(Irish)* Blond one

Boyne *(Irish)* White cow

Boynton *(Irish)* From the cold white river

Bozidar *(Russian)* God's gift

Brad *(Old English)* Broad

Bradburn *(Old English)* Broad brook

Braden *(Old English)* Wide valley

Bradford *(Old English)* From the broad river crossing

Bradley *(Old English)* From the broad meadow

Bradshaw *(Old English)* Big virgin forest

Bradwell *(Old English)* Broad stream

Brady *(Irish)* One with spirit

Brae *(Scottish)* Hill

Brainard *(Old English)* Bold raven

Bram *(Irish)* Raven. *Short for* Abraham

Bramwell *(Old English)* Abraham's well

Bran *(Celtic)* Raven

Brand *(Old English)* Firebrand

Brander *(Old Norse)* Firebrand

Brandon *(Old English)* From the beacon hill

Brant *(Old English)* Proud

Brawley *(Old English)* From the meadow on the slope

Brendan *(Irish)* Little raven

Brent *(Old English)* Steep hill

Bret *See* Brett

Brett *(Celtic)* Briton

Brewster *(Old English)* Brewer

Brian *See* Bryan

Briano *(Italian)* Bryan

Briant *See* Bryan

Brice *(Welsh)* Quick/Ambitious

Brien *See* Bryan

Brigham *(Old English)* From the enclosed bridge

Brion *See* Bryan

Brock *(Old English)* Badger

Brockley *(Old English)* From the badger meadow

Broderick *(Middle English)* From the broad ridge

Brodie *(Irish)* Ditch

Brody *See* Brodie

Bromley *(Old English)* Broombrush meadow

Bronson *(Old English)* Son of a brown person

Brook *(Old English)* From the brook

Brougher *(Old English)* One who lives at the fortress

Broughton *(Old English)* From the fortress town

Bruce *(French)* From the thicket

Bruno *(Old German)* Brown

Bryan *(Irish)* Strength

Bryant *(Welsh)* Powerful

Bryce *See* Brice

Bryon *See* Bryan

Buck *(Old English)* Male deer

Buckley *(Old English)* Deer meadow

Bundy *(Old English)* Free man

Bunyan *(Australian Aboriginal)* Place of pigeons

Burch *(Middle English)* Birch tree

Burchard *(Old English)* Powerful as a castle

Burdett *(Old French)* Little shield

Burgaud *(French)* Burchard

Burgess *(Old English)* Inhabitant of a fortified town

Burke *(Old French)* Inhabitant of the fortress

Burkett *(Old French)*

Inhabitant of the little stronghold

Burkhart *(German)* Burchard

Burl *(Old English)* Cupbearer

Burleigh *(Old English)* Clearing with tree trunks

Burley *See* Burleigh

Burnard *See* Bernard

Burne *(Old English)* From the brook

Burns *(Scottish)* Streams

Burr *(Old Norse)* Youth

Burril *(Australian Aboriginal)* Wallaby

Burt *(Old English)* Bright

Burton *(Old English)* Inhabitant of the fortified town

Byford *(Old English)* One who lives at the river crossing

Byrd *(Old English)* Like a bird

Byrle *See* Burl

Byrne *See* Burne

Byron *(Old French)* Bearlike

C

Caddock *(Welsh)* Keen to do battle

Cadell *(Welsh)* Defence against war

Cadeyrn *(Welsh)* King of battle

Cadfan *(Welsh)* Battle peak

Cadfer *(Welsh)* Lord of battle

Cadman *(Welsh)* Warrior

Cadmus *(Greek)* Man from the East

Caesar *(Latin)* Long-haired

Cahill *(Irish)* Charles

Cailean *(Scottish)* Colin

Cain *(Hebrew)* One who is possessed

Cain *(Hebrew)* Possessed

Cal *See* Calvin

Calder *(Old English)* Stream/Brook

Caldwell *(Old English)* One who lives by the cold spring

Caleb *(Hebrew)* Bold

Caley *(Irish)* Slender build

Calhoun *(Irish)* Hero/Forest dweller

Callaghan *(Irish)* Strife

Callagun *(Australian Aboriginal)* Blue fig

Callum *(Scottish)* Follower of St Columb

Calvert *(Old English)* Herdsman

Calvin *(Latin)* Bald

Calvino *(Italian, Spanish)* Calvin

Cam *See* Cameron

Camden *(Irish)* Windy, winding valley

Cameron *(Irish)* Bent/Crooked nose

Campbell *(Gaelic)* Crooked mouth

Candido *(Latin)* White

Canute *(Scandinavian)* Knot

Carey *(Welsh)* Castle dweller

Carl *(German)* Charles

Carleton *(Old English)* From Charles's homestead

Carlin *(Irish)* Little champion

Carlisle *(Old English)* Castle/Fortified town

Carlos *(Spanish)* Charles

Carlton *See* Carleton

Carlyle *(Welsh)* Carlisle

Carmichael *(Irish)* From Michael's castle/Stronghold

Carmine *(Latin)* Song

Carney *(Irish)* Victorious

Carollan *(Irish)* Little champion

Carr *(Scandinavian)* From the marsh

Carrick *(Gaelic)* Rocky headland

Carson *(Middle English)* Son of the marsh-dweller

Carter *(Old English)* Cart driver

Cary *See* Carey

Casey *(Irish)* Brave

Casimir *(Polish)* Proclamation of peace

Casimiro *(Spanish)* Casimir

Caspar *See* Casper

Casper *(Persian)* Treasure

Cass *See* Casper

Cassidy *(Irish)* Clever

Castor *(Greek)* Beaver

Cathal *(Celtic)* Mighty in battle

Cato *(Latin)* Cautious

Cavan *(Irish)* Handsome

Cecil *(Latin)* Blind

Cecilius *(Dutch)* Cecil

Cedric *(Old English)* Battle leader

Cesar *See* Caesar

Cesare *(Italian)* Caesar

Chad *(Old English)* Warlike

Chaim *(Hebrew)* Life

Chalmer *(Old Scottish)* Head of the household

Chandler *(Middle English)* Candle maker

Chandra *(Sanskrit)* Moon

Chang Yen *(Chinese)* True word

Channing *(Old French)* High church official

Chapman *(Old English)* Trader/Merchant

Charampios *(Greek)* Joy

Charles *(Old German)* Manly

Charlton *(Old English)* From Charles' farm

Chen *(Chinese)* After the 6th Century dynasty

Cheney *(Old French)*

124

Inhabitant of the oak forest

Cheng *(Chinese)* Correct

Chester *(Old English)* One who lives in the fortified army camp

Chet *See* Chester

Chico *(Spanish) Diminutive of* Charles/Francisco

Chris *(English) Short for* Christian/Christopher

Christian *(Greek)* Follower of Christ

Christiano *(Italian)* Christian

Christof *(Russian)* Christopher

Christoffer *(Danish)* Christopher

Christophe *(French)* Christopher

Christopher *(Greek)* Bearer of Christ

Christophorus *(German)* Christopher

Chrysander *(Greek)*

Golden man

Chuck *(American) Familiar of* Charles

Claiborn *See* Clay

Clarence *(Latin)* Famous

Clark *(French)* Scholar

Clark *(Old French)* Scholar

Claude *(Latin)* Lame

Claudius *See* Claude

Clay *(Old English)* From the earth

Claybourne *See* Clay

Clayton *(Old English)* From the pottery

Cledwyn *(Welsh)* Blessed sword

Clement *(Latin)* Merciful/Gentle

Cleon *(Greek)* Famous

Cleveland *(Old English)* From the cliff-land

Clevon *See* Cleveland

Clifford *(Old English)*

River crossing at the cliffside

Clifton *(Old English)* Town near the cliff

Clint *See* Clinton

Clinton *(Old English)* From the hill/Hilltown

Clive *(Old English)* From the cliff

Clodoveo *(Spanish)* Clovis

Clovis *(Old German)* Famous warrior

Clunies *(Irish)* Meadow

Clydai *(Welsh)* Fame

Clyde *(Irish)* Rocky eminence

Cody *(Old English)* A cushion

Coen *(Australian Aboriginal)* Thunder

Cohen *(Hebrew)* Priest

Colby *(Old English)* Cole's farm/Black farm

Colin *(Irish)* Child

Compton *(Old English)* Place in the valley

Conan *(Irish)* Intelligent

Coniah *(Hebrew)* Gift from God

Conlan *(Irish)* Hero

Connor *(Irish)* High desire

Conrad *(Old German)* Bold and wise counsellor

Conroy *(Irish)* Wise person

Constant *See* Constantine

Constantine *(Latin)* Steadfast

Conway *(Irish)* Hound of the plain

Cooba *(Australian Aboriginal)* Tiny black bee

Cooper *(Old English)* Barrel maker

Corbett *(Old French)* Raven

Corbin *See* Corbett

Corby *See* Corbett

Corcoran *(Irish)* Ruddy complexion

Cordell *(Old French)* Ropemaker

Corey *(Irish)* One who lives by a hollow

Cormack *See* Cormick

Cormick *(Irish)* Charioteer

Cornel *See* Cornelius

Cornelius *(Latin)* Horn/Horn-coloured

Corydon *(Greek)* Lark

Cosimo *(Italian, Spanish)* Cosmo

Cosmo *(Greek)* Universe

Courtney *(Old French)* One who lives at the farmstead

Cowan *(Australian Aboriginal)* Expanse of water

Coyle *(Irish)* Battle follower

Craig *(Irish)* One who lives at the crag

Crawford *(Old English)* Ford of the crow

Creighton *(Middle English)* Inhabitant of the town at the creek

Crispin *(Latin)* Curly haired

Cristoforo *(Italian)* Christopher

Cromwell *(Old English)* One who lives at the winding stream

Cullen *(Irish)* Handsome

Culver *(Old English)* Dove

Curran *(Irish)* Hero

Currumbin *(Australian Aboriginal)* Pine tree

Curtis *(Old French)* Courteous

Cuthbert *(Old English)* Famous

Cyrano *(Greek)* From Cyrene

Cyril *(Greek)* Lord

Cyrus *(Old Persian)* The sun

D

D'Arcy *(Old French)*
From the fortress

Dacey *(Irish)* Southerner

Dag *(Old Norse)* Day

Dalbert *(Old English)*
Proud

Dale *(Old English)* One
who lives in the valley

Dallas *(Irish)*
Wise/Skillful

Dalman *(Australian
Aboriginal)* Place of
plenty

Dalton *(Old English)*
From the town in the
dale

Daly *(Irish)* Counsellor

Damek *(Czech)* Man of
the red earth

Damian *See* Damon

Damien *See* Damon

Damon *(Greek)* To tame

Dan *(Hebrew)* Judge.
Short for Daniel

Dana *(Old English)*
From Denmark

Daniel *(Hebrew)* God is
my judge

Dante *(Italian)* Lasting

Darby *(Irish)* Free man

Darcy *See* D'Arcy

Darius *(Greek)* Wealthy

Darnell *(Old English)*
From the hidden hollow

Darrel *(French)* Beloved

Darrell *See* Darrel

Darren *(Irish)* Great

Darrill *See* Darrel

Daryl *See* Darrel

David *(Hebrew)* Beloved

Davin *(Scandinavian)*
Bright person from
Finland

Davis *(Old English)* Son
of David

Dean *(Old English)* One
who lives in the valley

Dedrick *(Old German)*

Ruler

Delaney *(Irish)* Descendant of the challenger

Delano *(Old French)* Of the night

Delbert *(Old English)* Bright as day

Delmar *(Latin)* From the sea

Delwyn *(Old English)* Proud friend

Demas *(Greek)* Popular person

Demetrius *(Greek)* Belonging to the goddess of fertility

Demos *(Greek)* The people

Demosthenes *(Greek)* Strength of the people

Dempsey *(Irish)* Proud

Dempster *(Old English)* The judge

Denis *See* Dennis

Denman *(Old English)* Resident of the valley

Dennis *(Greek)* Follower of the god of wine, Dionysos

Dennison *(Old English)* Son of Dennis

Denzil *(Cornish)* High stronghold

Deon *See* Dennis

Derain *(Australian Aboriginal)* Mountain

Derek *(Old German)* Ruler of the people

Dermot *(Irish)* Free man

Derrick *See* Derek

Derry *(Irish)* Red-haired

Derryn *(Welsh)* Little bird

Derwin *(Old English)* Beloved friend

Desmond *(Irish)* Man from south Munster

Devlin *(Irish)* Fierce

Dewey *(Welsh)* Prized/Beloved

Dexter *(Latin)* Right-handed

Dhatri *(Sanskrit)* Creator

Dick *See* Richard

Diego *(Spanish)* Jacob

Dieter *(German)* Strong person

Digby *(Old Norse)* Farm at the ditch

Dillon *(Irish)* Faithful

Dino *(Italian)* Dean

Dirk *See* Theodore

Dixon *(Old English)* Son of Richard

Djuro *(Yugoslavian)* George

Dmitri *(Russian)* Demetrius

Dolf *See* Adolph

Dolph *See* Adolph

Domingo *(Spanish)* Dominic

Dominic *(Latin)* Belonging to the Lord

Donahue *(Irish)* Dark/Brown warrior

Donald *(Celtic)* World ruler

Donato *(Latin)* Gift

Donovan *(Celtic)* Dark warrior

Doongara *(Australian Aboriginal)* Lightning

Dorak *(Australian Aboriginal)* Lively

Doran *(Greek)* A gift

Dorcas *(Hebrew)* From the forest

Dorian *(Greek)* One from the sea

Dorien *See* Dorian

Dougal *(Old Irish)* Black stranger

Douglas *(Celtic)* Dark water

Dov *(Hebrew)* David

Dow *(Irish)* Black-haired

Doyle *(Irish)* Dark stranger

Dragan *(Slavonic)* Dear

Drake *(Old English)* Dragon

Drew *(Old Welsh)* Wise one. *Also Short for* Andrew

Driscoll *(Irish)* One who

interprets

Druce *(Welsh)* Wise man's son

Drummond *(Celtic)* Dweller on the hilltop

Drury *(Old French)* Sweetheart

Dryden *(Old English)* From the dry valley

Duane *(Irish)* Small and dark

Duarte *(Portuguese)* Edward

Dudley *(Old English)* From the meadow

Dugan *(Irish)* Swarthy

Duke *(Old French)* Leader

Duncan *(Scottish)* Swarthy warrior

Dunley *(Old English)* From the hill meadow

Dunmore *(Gaelic)* From the great hill fort

Durrebar *(Australian Aboriginal)* Black cockatoo

Durward *(Old English)* Guardian of the gate

Dustin *(Old German)* Valiant

Dwayne *See* Duane

Dwight *(Old Dutch)* White one

Dylan *(Old Welsh)* God from the sea

Dzik *(Polish)* Wild man

E

Eachan *(Irish)* Horseman

Eamon *(Irish)* Edmund

Earl *(Old English)* Nobleman

Eben *(Hebrew)* Stone

Ebenezer *(Hebrew)* Stone of help

Eberhard *(Old German)* Brave as a wild boar

Edan *(Celtic)* Fire

Edbert *(Old English)*

Prosperous

Edelmar (*Old English*) Noble

Eden *See* Aidan

Edgar (*Old English*) Fortunate spear carrier

Edgard (*French*) Edgar

Edgardo (*Italian*) Edgar

Edison (*Old English*) Edward's son

Edmond (*French, Dutch*) Edmund

Edmund (*Old English*) Fortunate protector

Edmundo (*Spanish*) Edmund

Edouard (*French*) Edward

Edrei (*Hebrew*) Strong leader

Edsel (*Old English*) Deep thinker

Eduard (*German, Dutch*) Edward

Eduardo (*Italian, Spanish, Portuguese*) Edward

Edvard (*Swedish, Danish*) Edward

Edward (*Old English*) Prosperous protector

Edwin (*Old English*) Rich and fortunate friend

Egan (*Irish*) Fiery and ardent person

Egbert (*Old English*) Bright as a sword

Ehren (*Old German*) Honourable person

Ehud (*Hebrew*) Praise

Eirenaios (*Greek*) Peaceful

Eirig (*Welsh*) Happy

Eiros (*Welsh*) Bright

Eisak (*Russian*) Laughter

Elbert *See* Albert

Eldad (*Hebrew*) Beloved of God

Elden *See* Alden

Elder (*Old English*) One who lives at the elder tree

Eldin *See* Alden

Eldred *(Old English)* Wise/Old counsellor

Eldric *See* Aldrich

Eldwin *(Old English)* Old friend

Eleazar *(Hebrew)* To whom God is a help

Elgar *(Old English)* Noble spear carrier

Eli *(Hebrew)* Highest

Elijah *(Hebrew)* Jehovah is my God

Elisha *(Hebrew)* God is my salvation

Ellard *(Old German)* Noble and brave

Ellery *(Old English)* One who lives by the elder tree

Elliot *See* Elijah

Ellis *See* Elijah

Ellison *(Old English)* Son of Ellis

Elmer *(Old English)* Noble and famous

Elmo *(Greek)* Friendly

Elmore *(Old English)* One who lives at the elm-tree moor

Elroy *(Spanish)* King

Elsworth *(Old English)* Noble one's estate

Elton *(Old English)* One from the old farm or town

Elvis *(Old English)* Noble elf

Elwin *(Old English)* Holy friend

Elwood *(Old English)* One from the old forest

Emanuele *(Italian)* Emmanual

Emerson *(Old English)* Son of Emery

Emery *(Old German)* Hardworking ruler

Emil *(Latin)* One who flatters

Emlyn *(Welsh)* One who lives at the border

Emmanual *(Hebrew)* God with us

Emry *(Welsh)* Honour

Endor *(Hebrew)* From the fountain of youth

Eneas *(Spanish)* Aeneas

Engelbert *(Old German)* Bright as an angel

Engenius *(Dutch)* Eugene

Enne *(French)* Aeneas

Ennis *(Irish)* Only choice

Enoch *(Hebrew)* Consecrated

Enrico *(Italian)* Henry

Enrique *(Spanish)* Henry

Ephraim *(Hebrew)* Extremely fruitful

Erasmus *(Greek)* Lovable/Desired

Erberto *(Italian)* Herbert

Erhard *(Old German)* Strong/Resolute

Eric *(Old Norse)* Ever powerful

Erich *(German)* Eric

Erik *(Scandinavian)* Eric

Ermanno *(Italian)* Herman

Ernest *(Old English)* Earnest one

Ernesto *(Italian, Spanish)* Ernest

Ernestus *(Dutch)* Ernest

Ernst *(German)* Ernest

Errol *(Old English)* A wanderer

Erskine *(Scottish)* From the clifftop

Erwin *(Old English)* Friend of the army

Esbern *(Danish)* Holy bear

Esdras *(Hebrew)* Help

Esko *(Finnish)* Leader

Esmond *(Old English)* Gracious protector

Esteban *(Spanish)* Stephen

Etienne *(French)* Stephen

Ettore *(Italian)* Hector

Euclid *(Greek)* True glory

Eugen *(German)* Eugene

Eugene *(Greek)* Noble

Eugenic *(Italian, Spanish, Portuguese)* Eugene

Eusebuis *(Greek)* Honourable

Evan *(Celtic)* Young warrior. *Also (Welsh)* John

Everard *(Old English)* Brave as a boar

Everardo *(Italian)* Everard

Everett *See* Everard

Everhart *(Dutch)* Everard

Evraud *(French)* Everard

Ewald *(Old English)* Powerful

Ewen *(Celtic)* Noble youth

Ewert *(Old English)* Ewe-herder

Ewing *(Old English)* Lawyer and friend

Ezekiel *(Hebrew)* Strength of God

Ezra *(Hebrew)* Helper

F

Fabian *(Latin)* Bean-grower

Fabien *(French)* Fabian

Fabio *(Italian)* Fabian

Fadil *(Arabic)* Generous

Fagan *(Irish)* Small and fiery person

Fagin *See* Fagan

Fairfax *(Old English)* One with light hair

Falkner *(Old English)* Trainer of falcons

Farley *(Old English)* Meadow with ferns/Sheep

Farnham *(Old English)* From the field of ferns

Farouk *(Arabic)* A person who knows right from wrong

Farquhar *(Irish)* Friendly

Farrell *(Irish)* Heroic

Faust *See* Faustus

Faustus *(Latin)* Fortunate

Favian *(Latin)* Understanding

Fay (Irish) Raven

Fazio *(Italian)* Good worker

Federico *(Spanish)* Frederick

Federigo *(Italian)* Frederick

Fedor *(Russian)* Theodore

Felicius *(Latin)* Happier

Felipe *(Spanish)* Philip

Felix *(Latin)* Fortunate/Happy

Fenton *(Old English)* Town near the marsh

Feodor *(Slavic)* Theodore

Ferdinand *(Old German)* Adventurous

Ferdinando *(Italian)* Ferdinand

Ferenc *(Hungarian)* Francis

Fergal *(Irish)* Strong man

Fergus *See* Fergal

Fermac *(Irish)* Bright man

Fermin *(Spanish)* Firm

Fernando *(Spanish, Italian)* Ferdinand

Ferris *(Irish)* The Rock

Fidel *(Latin)* Faithful

Fidele *(French)* Fidel

Fidelio *(Italian)* Fidel

Fielding *(Old English)* From the field

Filbert *(Old English)* Brilliant

Filmer *See* Filmore

Filmore *(Old English)* Famous

Finbar *(Celtic)* One with a fair head

Findlay *(Celtic)* Fair hero

Finlay *See* Findlay

Finley *See* Findlay

136

Finn *(Irish)* Fairhaired/Fair-complexioned

Fiorello *(Latin)* Little flower

Firdaus *(Indonesian)* Paradise

Fisk *(Norse)* Fish

Fitz *(Old English)* Son of ...

Fitzgerald *(Old English)* Son of Gerald

Fitzhugh *(Old English)* Son of the clever man/Son of Hugh

Fitzpatrick *(Old English)* Son of a nobleman/Son of Patrick

Fitzroy *(French)* Son of the king

Flan *(Irish)* Red-haired

Flavio *(Italian)* Blonde one

Fletcher *(Middle English)* One who makes or feathers arrows

Florian *(Latin)* Flowering/Flourishing

Floyd *See* Lloyd

Flynn *(Irish)* Son of a redhaired man/Son of Finn

Forbes *(Irish)* Prosperous

Ford *(Old English)* River crossing

Francesco *(Italian)* Francis

Francis *(Latin)* Frenchman/Free man

Francisco *(Spanish)* Francis

Francois *(French)* Francis

Frane *(Yugoslavian)* Francis

Frank *Diminutive of Francis*

Franklin *(Middle English)* Free landowner

Frans *(Swedish)* Francis

Frants *(Danish)* Francis

Franz *(German)* Francis

Frazer *(Old English)*

One with curly hair

Frederick *(Old German)*
Peaceful ruler

Freeman *(Old English)*
Free-born man

Fremont *(Old German)*
One who guards
freedom

Frewin *(Old English)*
Free and noble friend

Friedrich *(German)*
Frederick

Fritz *See* Frederick

Fu Chung *(Chinese)*
Royal person

Fu *(Chinese)* Happiness

Fudo *(Japanese)* God of
fire/Wisdom

FuHai *(Chinese)*
Happiness as plentiful
as the eastern sea

Fulbert *(Old German)*
Bright

Fyfe *(Scottish)* From
Fifeshire in Scotland

Fyodor *(Russian)*
Theodore

G

Gable *(Old French)* Little
Gabriel

Gabor *(Hungarian)*
Gabriel

Gabriel *(Hebrew)* Man
of God

Gabriello *(Italian)*
Gabriel

Gabryel *(Polish)* Gabriel

Gage *(Old French)*
Pledge

Gailard *See* Gaylord

Galen *(Irish)* Little
bright one

Galeran *(French)*
Healthy rule

Galeus *(Greek)* Lizard

Gallagher *(Irish)* Eager
helper

Galloway *(Old Gaelic)*
Man from the land of
the stranger Gaels

Galvin *(Irish)* Sparrow

Gamaliel *(Hebrew)* God's recompense

Gamel *(Scandinavian)* Old

Ganan *(Australian Aboriginal)* West

Gandolf *(German)* Progress of the wolf

Garalt *(French)* Gerald

Gardner *(Middle English)* Gardener

Gareth *(Welsh)* Gentle

Garfield *(Old Engiish)* Battlefield

Garland *(Old English)* From the land of spears

Garman *(Old English)* Spearman

Garner *(Old French)* Military guard

Garnett *(Old English)* One armed with a spear

Garrett *(Irish)* Gerard

Garrick *(Old English)* Oak spear

Garth *(Old Norse)* Grounds keeper

Garvey *(Irish)* Rough peace

Garwin *See* Garvey

Gary *(Old English)* Spear carrier

Gaspar *(Persian)* Keeper of the treasure

Gaspard *(French)* Gaspar

Gasparo *(Italian)* Gaspar

Gaston *(French)* Man from Gascony

Gautama *(Sanskrit)* Name of the Buddha

Gautier *(French)* Walter

Gautrek *(Swedish)* Gothic king

Gautulf *(Swedish)* Gothic wolf

Gavin *(Welsh)* White hawk

Gavra *(Slavonic)* Hero of God

Gawain *(Welsh)* Hawk

Gayadin *(Australian*

Aboriginal) Platypus

Gayler *See* Gaylord

Gaylord *(Old French)* Lively one

Gazza *(Australian)* Gary

Gearalt *(Irish)* Gerald

Gearard *See* Gearalt

Geary *(Middle English)* One who changes

Geert *(Dutch)* Gerard

Gelasius *(Greek)* Laughter

Gellies *(Dutch)* One who makes war

Geno *(Italian)* John

Gentile *(Italian)* Kind

Geoffredo *(Italian)* Geoffrey

Geoffrey *(English)* Godfrey. *Also (Old German)* God's peace

Geoffroi *(French)* Geoffrey

Georas *(Scottish)* George

Georg *(Danish, German,*

Swedish) George

George *(Greek)* Farmer

Georges *(French)* George

Georgios *(Greek)* George

Geraint *(Welsh)* Old

Gerald *(Old German)* Spear ruler

Gerard *(Old English)* Brave spear carrier

Gerardo *(Spanish)* Gerard

Geraud *(French)* Gerard

Geremia *(Italian)* Jeremiah

Gerhardt *(German)* Gerard

Gerold *(German)* Gerald

Geronimo *(Italian)* Jerome

Gershom *(Hebrew)* Exile

Gervase *(Old German)* Honourable

Gerwyn *(Welsh)* Fair love

Gethin *(Welsh)*
Dark-skinned

Ghafur *(Arabic)* One
who forgives

Ghazzali *(Arabic)* Proof
of Islam

Ghislaine *(French)*
Pledge

Giacobbe *(Italian)* Jacob

Giacobo *See* Jacob

Gian *(Italian)* John

Gibson *(Old English)*
Son of Gilbert

Gideon *(Hebrew)*
Destroyer

Gifford *(Old English)*
Bold giver

Gilbert *(Old English)*
Trust/Pledge

Gilberto *(Italian)* Gilbert

Gilchrist *(Irish)* Servant
of Christ

Giles *(Greek)* Shield
carrier

Gilibeirt *(Irish)* Gilbert

Gilleabart *(Scottish)*
Gilbert

Gilles *(French)* Giles

Gilmer *(Old English)*
Famous hostage

Gilmore *(Celtic)*
Follower of the Virgin
Mary

Gilroy *(Irish)* Devoted to
the king

Gino *(Italian) Short for*
Ambrogio

Giobbe *(Italian)* Job

Giocopo *(Italian)* Jacob

Gioffredo *(Italian)*
Geoffrey

Giordano *(Italian)*
Jordan

Giorgio *(Italian)* George

Gioseffa *(Italian)* Joseph

Giovanni *(Italian)* John

Giraldo *(Italian)* Gerald

Giraud *(French)* Gerald

Girra *(Australian
Aboriginal)* Creek

Girvin *(Irish)* Little
rough one

Giselbert *(German)*

141

Gilbert

Giuliano *(Italian)* Julian

Giulio *(Italian)* Jules

Giuseppe *(Italian)* Joseph

Giustino *(Italian)* Justin

Giusto *(Italian)* Justice

Gladwin *(Old English)* Glad friend

Glanville *(Old French)* From the estate with oak trees

Glen *(Irish)* Valley

Glynne *(Welsh)* Glen

Godard *(French)* Goddard

Goddard *(Old German)* Firm in God

Godefroi *(French)* Godfrey

Godewyn *(Dutch)* Godwin

Godfrey *(Old German)* Divine and peaceful

Godofredo *(Spanish)* Godfrey

Godwin *(Old English)* God's friend

Goffredo *(Italian)* Godfrey

Golding *(Old English)* Son of the golden one

Goldwin *(Old English)* Golden friend

Gomer *(Hebrew)* To finish

Gomez *(Spanish)* Man

Gonsalvo *(Italian)* Gonzales

Gonzales *(Spanish)* Warlike wolf

Goodman *(Old English)* Good man

Goolcoola *(Australian Aboriginal)* Sweet

Goonagulla *(Australian Aboriginal)* Sky

Goonaroo *(Australian Aboriginal)* Whistling duck

Goraidh *(Scottish)* Godfrey

142

Gordon *(Old English)* Great hill

Gorman *(Irish)* Little one with blue eyes

Goronwy *(Welsh)* Old

Gothfraidh *(Irish)* Godfrey

Gottfrid *(Swedish)* Godfrey

Gottfried *(German)* Godfrey

Gotthard *(Dutch)* Goddard

Gotthart *(German)* Goddard

Gough *(Welsh)* Red-haired person

Gower *(Old Welsh)* Pure one

Grady *(Irish)* Illustrious/ Noble

Graeme *(Old English)* Gray home

Graham *See* Graeme

Granger *(Old English)* Farmer

Grant *(French)* Great

Granville *(French)* Big place/Town

Gray *(Old English)* Grey-coloured

Greagoir *(Irish)* Gregory

Gregoire *(French)* Gregory

Gregoor *(Dutch)* Gregory

Gregorio *(Italian, Spanish)* Gregory

Gregorios *See* Gregory

Gregorius *(German)* Gregory

Gregory *(Greek)* Watchful/Vigilant

Greig *(Scottish)* Gregory

Griffin *(Welsh)* Staunchly faithful

Griffith *(Celtic)* Red-haired

Griogair *(Scottish)* Gregory

Grover *(Old English)* From the grove of trees

Gualtiero *(Italian)* Walter

Guglielmo *(Italian)*
William

Guido *(Italian)* Guy

Guilbert *(French)* Gilbert

Guillaume *(French)*
William

Guillermo *(Spanish)*
William

Guin *(Gaelic)* Gwynne

Guiseppe *(Italian)*
Joseph

Gunther *(Old German)*
Battle army

Gurion *(Hebrew)* God's
dwelling

Gustaf *See* Gustavius

Gustav *See* Gustavius

Gustavius *(Old
German)* God's staff

Guthrie *(Old German)*
Heroic warrior

Guy *(French)* Guide

Gwilyn *(Welsh)* William

Gwynne *(Welsh)* White

Gyorgy *(Hungarian)*
George

H

Haakon *(Scandinavian)*
Noble relative

Habakkuk *(Hebrew)*
Embrace

Habib *(Arabic)* Beloved

Hadden *(Old English)*
From the heath-valley

Hadleigh *See* Hadley

Hadley *(Old English)*
From the heath meadow

Hadrian *See* Adrian

Hafiz *(Arabic)* He who
remembers

Hagan *(Irish)* Small and
youthful

Hagar *(Hebrew)*
Forsaken

Hai *(Chinese)* The sea

Haig *(Old English)* Field
surrounded by hedges

Hakeem *(Arabic)* Wise

Hakon *(Old Norse)* Of

noble extraction

Hal *See* Harold

Hale *(Old English)* Hero

Haley *(Irish)* Ingenious

Hallam *(Old English)* One who lives on the slopes

Halliwell *(Old English)* One who lives by a holy spring

Hamal *(Arabic)* Lamb

Hamid *(Arabic)* Thanks to God

Hamilton *(Old English)* Home-lover

Hamish *(Scottish)* Jacob

Hamlet *(Old French)* Little home

Hamon *(Greek)* Faithful

Hanif *(Arabic)* True believer

Hanley *(Irish)* Warrior

Hannibal *(Phoenician)* Grace of Baal

Hannu *(Finnish)* John

Hanraoi *(Irish)* Heinrich

Hans *(German)* John

Harald *(Danish, Swedish)*

Harailt *(Scottish)* Harold

Harden *(Old English)* From the valley with hares

Harding *(Old English)* Son of a brave man

Hardy *(Old German)* Tough

Hari *(Sanskrit)* He who removes sin

Harley *(Old English)* From the meadow with hares

Harman *See* Herman

Harold *(Old Norse)* Ruler of the army

Haroun *(Arabic)* High mountain

Harper *(Old English)* Harp player

Harris *(Old English)* Henry's son

Harrison *(Old English)* Harry's son

Harry *See* Harold/Henry

Hartert *See* Herbert

Hartley *(Old English)* Pasture of the hart deer

Hartman *(Old German)* Strong, tough man

Harun *(Arabic)* Exalted one

Harvey *(Old German)* Warrior

Hashim *(Arabic)* One who destroys evil

Hashum *(Hebrew)* Rich

Hassan *(Arabic)* Handsome

Hastings *(Old English)* Son of the violent man

Havelock *(Welsh)* Oliver

Hayden *(Old English)* From the hedged valley

Hayward *(Old English)* Protector of the hedged area

Haywood *(Old English)* From the forest surrounded by hedges

Hazael *(Hebrew)* Whom God sees

Hearn *See* Ahern

Hearne *See* Ahearn

Heath *(Middle English)* Field with heather

Heber *(Hebrew)* Associate

Hector *(Greek)* Steadfast

Hedley *(Old English)* Blessed peace

Heikki *(Finnish)* Heinrich

Hein *(Dutch)* Heinrich

Heine *See* Heinrich

Heinrich *(Old German)* Headman

Heinz *See* Heinrich

Helmut *(German)* Famous for courage

Hemi *(Maori)* Jacob

Hendrik *(Dutch, Danish)* Heinrich

Henri *(French)* Heinrich

Henrik *(Swedish)* Heinrich

Henrique *(Portuguese)* Heinrich

Henry (*English*) Heinrich

Herbert (*Old German*) Brilliant soldier

Hercules (*Greek*) Glorious gift

Herman (*Old German*) Warrior

Hernando (*Spanish*) Ferdinand

Herold (*Dutch*) Harold

Herrick (*Old German*) Army ruler

Hershel (*Hebrew*) Deer

Hervey *See* Harvey

Hewe *See* Hugh

Hewett (*Old French*) Little Hugh

Hieronomo (*Spanish*) Jerome

Hiew (*Vietnamese*) Pious one

Hilaire (*French*) Cheerful

Hillel (*Hebrew*) Greatly praised

Hilton (*Old English*) Town on the hill

Hiram (*Hebrew*) Most noble

Hjalmar (*Scandinavian*) Glorious helmet

Ho (*Chinese*) River

Hoa (*Vietnamese*) Peace-loving

Hodaka (*Japanese*) Mountain

Hogan (*Irish*) Youth

Hoibeard (*Irish*) Hubert

Holmes (*Middle English*) From the island in the river

Homer (*Greek*) Promise

Horace (*Latin*) Timekeeper

Hori (*Polynesian*) George

Horst (*German*) Thicket

Horton (*Latin*) Gardener

Hosea (*Hebrew*) Salvation

Houston (*Old English*) Hill town

Howard (*Old English*) Head guardian

147

Howe *(Old German)* Of high birth

Howell *(Welsh)* Eminent

Hradek *(Slavonic)* One who lives near a small castle

Hribar *(Slavonic)* One who lives on a hill

Hu *(Chinese)* Tiger

Hubert *(Old German)* Brilliant (intellect)

Huberto *(Spanish)* Hubert

Hudson *(Old English)* Son of the hooded one

Huey *See* Hugh

Hugh *(Old English)* Intelligent

Hugibert *(German)* Hubert

Hugo *See* Hugh

Hugues *(French)* Hugo

Hulbard *See* Hulbert

Hulbert *(Old German)* Graceful and clever

Humberto *(Spanish)* Giant

Humfrey *See* Humphrey

Humfrid *(Swedish)* Humphrey

Humfried *(German)* Humphrey

Humphrey *(Old German)* Peaceful Hun

Hunfredo *(Spanish)* Humphrey

Hung *(Vietnamese)* Strong

Hurley *(Irish)* Sea-tide

Hurst *(Middle English)* Forest dweller

Hussein *(Arabic)* Handsome and small

Huw *(Welsh)* Hugh

Huxford *(Old English)* Hugh's river crossing

Huxley *(Old English)* Hugh's meadow

Hyatt *(Old English)* From the high gate

I

I Chih *(Chinese)* Honourable/Intelligent

Iago *(Spanish)* Jacob

Iain *See* Ian

Ian *(Scottish)* John

Ibn *(Arabic)* Son of ...

Ibrahim *(Arabic)* Abraham

Ifan *(Welsh)* John

Ignace *(French)* Ignatius

Ignacio *(Spanish)* Ignatius

Ignatius *(Latin)* Ardent

Ignatz *See* Ignatius

Ignaz *(German)* Ignatius

Ignazio *(Italian)* Ignatius

Igor *(Russian)* Ingemar

Ihorangi *(Polynesian)* Rain

Ike *See* Isaac

Ilya *(Russian)* Jehovah is God

Ilyas *(Arabic)* Elijah

Immanuel *See* Emmanual

Ingemar *(Old Norse)* Famous son

Inger *(Old Norse)* A son's army

Ingmar *See* Ingemar

Ingram *(Old English)* Angel/Wisdom

Inigo *(Welsh)* Ignatius

Inir *(Welsh)* Honour

Innes *(Irish)* Island

Innis *See* Innes

Ion *See* John

Ira *(Hebrew)* On guard

Irvin *(Celtic)* White river

Irving *(Irish)* Handsome

Irwin *See* Irving

Isa *(Sanskrit)* Lord

Isaac *(Hebrew)* He who laughs

Isaak *(German, Russian)* Isaac

Isacco *(Italian)* Isaac

Isaiah *(Hebrew)* Jehovah is generous/The Lord is my Saviour

Ishmael *(Hebrew)* Wanderer

Isidore *(Greek)* Gift of Isis

Isidoro *(Italian)* Isidore

Isidro *(Spanish)* Isidore

Israel *(Hebrew)* Ruler with the Lord

Ithel *(Welsh)* Generous lord

Ithnan *(Hebrew)* Strong sailor

Ittamar *(Hebrew)* Island of palms

Ivan *(Russian)* John

Ivar *(Old Norse)* Archer with a yew bow

Ives *(Old English)* Archer

Ivor *(Welsh)* John

Izaak *(Dutch)* Isaac

J

Jabbar *(Arabic)* Repairer

Jacinto *(Spanish)* Purple hyacinth

Jack *See* John

Jackie *See* John

Jackson *(Old English)* Son of Jack

Jacob *(Hebrew)* Supplanter

Jacobo *(Spanish)* Jacob

Jacques *(French)* Jacob

Jago *(Australian Aboriginal)* Complete

Jahdal *(Hebrew)* Directed by God

Jair *(Hebrew)* He will enlighten

Jake *See* Jacob

Jakob *(German)* Jacob

Jakobus *(Greek)* Jacob

Jalil *(Arabic)* Majestic

James *See* Jacob

Jamil *(Arabic)* Handsome

Jan *(Dutch, Polish)* John

Janos *(Hungarian)* John

Jarvis *(Old German)* War-leader

Jascha *(Russian)* Jacob

Jason *(Greek)* Healer

Jasper *(Persian)* Guardian of the treasure

Jay *(English)* The bird

Jayme *(Old Spanish)* Jacob

Jean *(French)* John

Jed *See* Jedidiah

Jedidiah *(Hebrew)* Beloved of God

Jeff *See* Jeffrey

Jefferson *(Old English)* Son of Jeffrey

Jeffrey *(Old French)* Divine peace

Jens *(Danish)* Jacob

Jeremiah *(Hebrew)* Chosen by Jehovah

Jeremias *(Spanish)* Jeremiah

Jeremy *See* Jeremiah

Jerome *(Latin)* Holy name

Jervis *(German)* Spear carrier

Jesse *(Hebrew)* Rich

Jesus *(Hebrew)* God will help

Jevon *(Welsh)* John

Jim *See* Jacob

Joachim *(Hebrew)* May God exalt

Joan *(Rumanian)* John

Joao *(Brazilian)* John

Job *(Hebrew)* Persecuted

Jock *(Scottish)* Jack

Joe *See* Joseph

Joel *(Hebrew)* Jehovah is God

Joffre *(French)* Geoffrey

Johann *(German)* John

Johannes *(Dutch)* John

John *(Hebrew)* God is gracious

Jonah *(Hebrew)* Dove

Jonathan *(Hebrew)* Gift from God

Jordan *(Hebrew)* One who descends

Jorge *(Spanish)* George

Joris *(Dutch)* George

Jose *(Spanish)* Joseph

Josep *(Irish)* Joseph

Joseph *(Hebrew)* God has added a child

Josh *See* Joshua

Joshua *(Hebrew)* God is my helper

Josip *(Yugoslavian)* Joseph

Jourdain *(French)* Jordan

Jozef *(Hungarian)* Joseph

Juan *(Spanish)* John

Judd *(Hebrew)* Praised. *Also modern form of* Judah

Jules *See* Julius

Julian *(Latin)* Belonging to Julius

Julio *(Spanish)* Jules

Julius *(Latin)* Young

Juste *(French)* Justin

Justice *(Old French)* Judge

Justin *(Latin)* Justice

Justino *(Spanish)* Justin

Justis *(Old French)* Justice

Justo *(Spanish)* Justice

Justus *See* Justis

K

Kadumba *(Australian Aboriginal)* Waterfall

Kalil *(Arabic)* Good friend

Kambara *(Australian Aboriginal)* Crocodile

Kane *(Welsh)* Beautiful

Kareem *(Arabic)* Noble

Karel *(Dutch)* Charles

Karim *See* Kareem

Karl *(German)* Charles

Kasimir *(German)*

Casimir

Kavan *See* Cavan

Kay *(Old Welsh)* One who rejoices

Kayne *See* Kane

Keane *(Middle English)* Bold. *Also (Irish)* Handsome

Kedar *(Arabic)* Strong

Keefe *(Irish)* Enjoyment

Keegan *(Irish)* Small and fiery person

Keelan *(Irish)* Slender

Keeley *(Irish)* Handsome

Keenan *(Irish)* Little ancient one

Keith *(Irish)* From the battlefield

Keller *(Irish)* Little companion

Kelly *(Irish)* Warrior

Kelsey *(Old Norse)* One who lives at the island of ships

Kelvan *See* Kelvin

Kelven *See* Kelvin

Kelvin *(Irish)* Narrow river

Kemp *(Middle English)* Warrior

Ken *See* Kendal

Kendal *(Celtic)* Chief of the valley

Kendrick *(Irish)* Son of Henry

Kenn *(Old Welsh)* Bright and clear water

Kennard *(Old English)* Strong

Kennedy *(Irish)* Helmeted chief

Kenneth *(Irish)* Handsome

Kenrick *(Old English)* Bold ruler

Kent *(Old Welsh)* White/Bright

Kenyon *(Irish)* Blond

Kermit *(Irish)* Free

Kerr *(Celtic)* Dark

Kerry *(Irish)* Dark-haired

Kester (*Old English*)
From the Roman army
camp

Kev *See* Kevin

Kevin (*Irish*) Gentle

Key (*Irish*) Son of the
fiery one

Khalif (*Arabic*) King

Khalil (*Arabic*) Friend

Khegub (*Australian
Aboriginal*) Tree

Kienan *See* Keenan

Kieran (*Irish*) Small and
darkskinned

Kiernan *See* Kieran

Killian (*Irish*) Small and
warlike

Kim (*Old English*) Chief

Kimba (*Australian
Aboriginal*) Bush fire

Kimball (*Old English*)
Leader of warriors

Kincaid (*Celtic*) Battle
chief

King (*Old English*) Ruler

Kingsley (*Old English*)
From the king's wood or
meadow

Kingston (*Old English*)
From the king's estate

Kingswell (*Old English*)
One who lives at the
king's spring

Kinnard (*Irish*) From the
high hill

Kipp (*Old English*) From
the pointed hill

Kirby (*Old German*)
From the village with a
church

Kirk (*Norse*) Church

Kirkley (*Old English*)
Church meadow

Kirkwood (*Old English*)
From the church forest

Kit *See* Christopher

Kizil (*Turkish*) Red

Klaas (*Dutch*) Nicholas

Klaus (*German*) Nicholas

Knox (*Old English*) From
the hill

Knut (*Scandinavian*)
Canute

Koenraad *(Dutch)*
Conrad

Koiranah *(Australian Aboriginal)* Eagle

Konane *(Hawaiian)*
Bright moonlight

Konrad *See* Conrad

Kosey *(Swahili)* Lion

Kris *See*
Christian/Christopher

Krishna *(Hindi)*
Delightful

Kristian *(Swedish)*
Christian

Kristofor *(Swedish)*
Christopher

Kuei *(Chinese)* Spirit

Kuracca *(Australian Aboriginal)* Crestless white cockatoo

Kurao *(Japanese)*
Mountain

Kurt *(German)* Conrad

Kyle *(Irish)* From the strait

Kym *See* Kim

Kyne *(Old English)* Royal

L

Laban *(Hebrew)* White

Labhras *(Irish)*
Lawrence

Labhruinn *(Scottish)*
Lawrence

Lachlan *(Irish)* Warlike

Ladd *(Middle English)*
Young man/Attendant

Ladislas *(Slavic)* Glory

Lael *(Hebrew)* Belonging to the Lord

Laird *(Irish)* Lord

Lajos *(Hungarian)* Louis

Lambert *(Old German)*
Bright as the land

Lamberts *(Italian)*
Lambert

Lamech *(Hebrew)*
Strong youth

Lammond *See* Lamont

Lamont *(Old Norse)*
Lawyer

Lance *(Old French)* One who serves. *Short for* Lancelot

Landon *See* Langdon

Lane *(Middle English)* Narrow road

Lang *(Old Norse)* Long

Langdon *(Old English)* One who lives at the long hill

Larry *See* Lawrence

Lars *(Swedish)* Lawrence

Larson *(Scandinavian)* Son of Lars

Latham *(Old Norse)* From the barns

Latimer *(Middle English)* Interpreter

Laurence *See* Lawrence

Laurens *(Dutch)* Lawrence

Laurent *(French)* Lawrence

Laurenz *(German)* Lawrence

Lawford *(Old English)* From the ford at the hill

Lawley *(Old English)* From the meadow at the hill

Lawrence *(Latin)* Crowned with laurels

Lawson *(Old English)* Son of Lawrence

Lawton *(Old English)* From the hill-town

Lazare *(French)* Lazarus

Lazaro *(Italian, Spanish)* Lazarus

Lazarus *(Hebrew)* God will help

Leander *(Greek)* Like a lion

Lee *(Old English)* From the meadow

Leif *(Scandinavian)* Love

Leigh *See* Lee

Leith *(Scottish)* Wide river

Leland *(Old English)* Meadow-land

Lenard *See* Leonard

Lennard *See* Leonard

Lennon *(Irish)* Little

cloak

Lennox *(Celtic)* Chieftan

Leo *(Latin)* Lion

Leon *See* Leonard

Leonard *(Old Frankish)* Brave as a lion

Leonardo *(Italian)* Leonard

Leonhard *(German)* Leonard

Leonidas *(Greek)* Son of the lion

Leopold *(Old German)* Bold for the people

Leopoldo *(Italian, Spanish)* Leopold

Leroy *(Old French)* King

Leslie *(Celtic)* One who lives at the grey fortress

Lester *(Latin)* From the chosen camp

Lev *(Russian)* Leo

Leverett *(Old French)* Young rabbit

Levi *(Hebrew)* United

Lewis *(English)* Louis

Liam *(Irish)* William

Lincoln *(Old English)* From the colony by the pool

Lindbert *(Old German)* Linden tree hill

Lindley *(Old English)* At the linden tree meadow

Lindon *See* Lyndon

Lindsay *(Old English)* From the linden tree island

Lindsey *See* Lindsay

Linton *(Old English)* From the flax enclosure

Linus *(Greek)* One with flax-coloured hair

Lionel *(Old French)* Young lion

Lionello *(Italian)* Lionel

Lisle *(French)* Town

Livingston *(Old English)* From Leif's town

Lleufer *(Welsh)* Splendid

Llewellyn *(Old Welsh)* Like a lion

Lloyd *(Old Welsh)* Grey-haired

Locke *(Old English)* Lock

Lodewijk *(Dutch)* Louis

Lodovico *(Italian)* Louis

Logan *(Irish)* From the hollow

Lombard *(Latin)* One with a long beard

Lon *(Irish)* Strong

Lorant *(Hungarian)* Laurel tree

Loren *(Scandinavian)* Lawrence

Lorenz *(German)* Lawrence

Lorenzo *(Italian)* Lawrence

Lorimer *(Latin)* Harness-maker

Lorin *See* Lorant

Loring *(Old German)* Son of a famous warrior

Lorne *See* Lorant

Lotario *(Italian)* Luther

Lothaire *(French)* Luther

Louis *(Old German)* Famed warrior

Lourenco *(Portuguese)* Lawrence

Lovell *See* Lowell

Lowell *(Old French)* Little wolf

Luca *(Italian)* Luke

Lucas *(German)* Luke

Luciano *(Italian)* Luke

Lucien *(French)* Luke

Lucius *(Latin)* Light

Ludolf *(Old German)* Famous wolf

Ludvig *(Swedish)* Louis

Ludwig *(German)* Louis

Lugaidh *(Irish)* Louis

Luigi *(Italian)* Louis

Luis *(Spanish)* Louis

Luiz *(Portuguese)* Louis

Luke *(Latin)* Light

Lundy *(French)* Born on Monday

Lunn *(Irish)* Strong/Fierce

Lutero *(Spanish)* Luther

Luthais *(Scottish)* Louis

Luther *(Old German)* Famous/Renowned

Lycidas *(Greek)* Wolf son

Lyell *See* Lyle

Lyle *(Old French)* From the island

Lyndon *(Old English)* From the linden/Lime tree hill

Lynfa *(Welsh)* From the lake

M

Mac *(Celtic)* Son of ...

Macabee *(Hebrew)* Hammer

Macadam *(Old English)* Son of Adam

MacDonald *(Scottish)* Son of the world-mighty

MacDougall *(Scottish)* Son of the dark stranger

Macharios *(Greek)* Blessed

MacKinley *(Irish)* Skillful leader

MacMurray *(Irish)* Son of the seafarer

Maddock *See* Maddox

Maddox *(Welsh)* Fortunate

Madison *(Old English)* Powerful warrior

Madoc *(Welsh)* Fortunate

Magnus *(Latin)* Great

Mahamet *See* Mohomet

Majid *(Arabic)* Glorious

Major *(Latin)* Greater

Makarios *See* Macharios

Malachi *(Hebrew)* Messenger

Malcolm *(Celtic)* Disciple of St Columba

Malik *(Arabic)* Master

Mallory *(Old German)* Army advisor

Maloney *(Irish)*

Devoted to Sunday worship

Malvin *(Celtic)* Chief

Malvin *See* Melvin

Manchu *(Chinese)* Pure

Mandel *(German)* Almond

Manfred *(German)* Man of peace

Manning *(Old English)* Hero's son

Manny *See* Mandel

Manolis *(Greek)* God is with us

Mansfield *(Old English)* From the field by the small river

Manton *(Old English)* From the hero's estate

Manuel *(Spanish)* God with us

Maolmuire *(Scottish)* Maurice

Marc *(French)* Mark

Marcel *(Latin)* Little hammer

Marcello *(Italian)* Marcel

Marcellus *(French)* Marcel

Marcelo *(Spanish)* Marcel

Marco *(Spanish)/(Italian)* Mark

Marcos *(Spanish)* Marcus

Marcus *(Latin)* Warlike

Marden *(Old English)* From the pool-valley

Mariano *(Spanish)* Marion

Mario *(Italian)* Dedicated to the Virgin Mary

Marion *(Old French)* Masculine of Mary

Mark *See* Marcus

Markos *(Greek)* Mark

Markus *(German)* Mark

Marlin *See* Marlon

Marlon *(Old French)* Little falcon

Marlow *(Old English)* From the hill by the lake

Marmion *(Old French)* Very small one

Marsden *(Old English)* One who lives at the marshy valley

Marsdon *See* Marsden

Marsh *(Old English)* From the marshy place

Marshall *(Middle English)* Steward

Martainn *(Scottish)* Martin

Marten *See* Martin

Martijn *(Dutch)* Martin

Martin *(Latin)* Warlike

Martino *(Italian)* Martin

Marton *See* Martin

Marvin *(Old English)* One who loves the sea

Maslin *(Old French)* Little Thomas

Mason *(Old French)* Stonemason

Mata *(Scottish)* Matthew

Matareka *(Polynesian)* Smiling face

Mateo *(Spanish)* Matthew

Mathhaus *(German)* Matthew

Mathieu *(French)* Matthew

Matong *(Australian Aboriginal)* Powerful

Matteo *(Italian)* Matthew

Matthaeus *(Danish)* Matthew

Mattheus *(Swedish)* Matthew

Matthew *(Hebrew)* Gift from God

Matthias *(Greek)* Matthew

Matyas *(Hungarian)* Matthew

Maurice *(Latin)* Dark-skinned

Maurits *(Dutch)* Maurice

Maurizio *(Italian)* Maurice

Maximilian *(Latin)* Most excellent

Maxwell *(Old English)* From the well or spring of the influential man

Mayer *(Hebrew)* Light

Mayfield *(Old English)* From the warrior's field

Maynard *(Old German)* Powerful

Mayo *(Irish)* From the plain of the yew trees

Meldrick *(Old English)* Powerful mill

Melville *(Old French)* From the industrious one's estate

Melvin *(Old English)* Sword friend

Mendel *(Semitic)* Knowledge

Merce *See* Mercer

Mercer *(Middle English)* Merchant

Meredith *(Welsh)* Lord of the sea

Mereki *(Australian Aboriginal)* Peacemaker

Merlin *(Middle English)* Hawk

Mervin *(Old English)* Famous friend

Mervyn *See* Mervin

Meyer *(German)* Farmer

Michael *(Hebrew)* Who is like the Lord

Michan *(Irish)* Michael

Micheil *(Scottish)* Michael

Michel *(French)* Michael

Michele *(Italian)* Michael

Mickey *See* Michael

Midgee *(Australian Aboriginal)* Acacia tree

Miguel *(Spanish)* Michael

Mihai *(Rumanian)* Michael

Mihaly *(Hungarian)* Michael

Mikael *(Arabic, Swedish)* Michael

Mike *See* Michael

Milan *(Slavic)* Beloved

Miles *(Latin)* Soldier

Miloslav *(Slavic)* Crowned with glory

Milton *(Old English)* One who lives at the mill-town

Minh *(Vietnamese)* Light

Mirko *(Serbo-Croatian)* Michael

Mischa *(Slavic)* Michael

Mitch *See* Mitchell

Mitchell *See* Michael

Mohammed *See* Mohomet

Mohomet *(Arabic)* Glorified

Moise *See* Moses

Monroe *(Irish)* From the red swamp

Montague *(French)* Pointed mountain

Monte *(Latin)* Mountain

Montgomery *(French)* Mountain hunter

Moore *(French)* Dark-skinned

Moreland *(Old English)* From the moor-land

Morgan *(Celtic)* From the edge of the sea

Moriah *(Hebrew)* Chosen by Jehovah

Moritz *(German)* Maurice

Morley *(Old English)* From the moor meadow

Morris *See* Maurice

Morrison *(Old English)* Son of Maurice

Mortimer *(Old French)* From the still water

Morton *(Old English)* From the moor town

Morven *(Irish)* Fair-complexioned man

Moses *(Hebrew)* Saved from the water

Moshe *See* Moses

Mozes *(Dutch)* Moses

Muir *(Old English)* Moor

Mulga *(Australian Aboriginal)* Acacia

Mullion *(Australian Aboriginal)* Eagle

Muluk *(Indonesian)* Exalted

Mungo *(Irish)* Lovable

Murdoch *(Irish)*
Wealthy from the sea

Murdock *See* Murdoch

Murray *(Celtic)* Sailor

Musa *(Arabic)* Moses

Myer *(Hebrew)* Light

Myles *See* Miles

Myron *(Greek)* Fragrant

N

Naeem *(Arabic)*
Benevolent

Napoleon *(Italian)*
From Naples

Narcissus *(Greek)*
Self-loved

Natal *(Spanish, Portuguese)* Noel

Natale *(Italian)* Noel

Natanael *(Spanish)*
Nathaniel

Nathan *(Hebrew)* God's gift

Nathaniel *See* Nathan

Neacail *(Scottish)*
Nicholas

Neal *(Irish)* Champion

Ned *See* Edward

Nehemiah *(Hebrew)*
Consolation of God

Neil *See* Neal

Nelson *(Celtic)* Son of Neal

Nemo *(Greek)* From the glade

Nepo *(Australian Aboriginal)* Comrade

Nestor *(Greek)* Wise

Neumann *(German)*
New man

Neville *(Latin)* New town

Nevin *(Irish)*
Worshipper of the saint

Newell *(Old English)*
New

Newman *(Old English)*
Newcomer

Newton *(Old English)*
New town

Ngutuku *(Polynesian)* Fish

Nial *See* Niall

Niall *(Scottish)* Neal

Nicholas *(Greek)* Victory of the people

Nick *See* Nicholas

Nicolaas *(Dutch)* Nicholas

Nicolas *(Spanish)* Nicholas

Nicolo *(Italian)* Nicholas

Nigel *(Latin)* Black

Nikolai *(Slavic)* Nicholas

Nikolaus *(German)* Nicholas

Nils *(Scandinavian)* Neal

Nimrod *(Hebrew)* Brave/Valiant

Niven *(Irish)* Little saint

Nixon *(Old English)* Son of Nicholas

Noah *(Hebrew)* Long-lived

Noak *(Swedish)* Noah

Noam *(Hebrew)* Pleasant

Noble *(Latin)* Well-born

Noel *(French)* Born on Christmas Day

Nolan *(Irish)* Noble

Norbert *(German)* Famous northener

Norm *See* Norman

Norman *(Old French)* Norseman

Norris *(Old French)* Northener

Northcliff *(Old English)* From the north cliff

Northrop *(Old English)* From the northern farm

Norton *(Old English)* From the northern town

Norwood *(Old English)* North wood

Nowell *See* Noel

Nuri *(Hebrew)* Fire

O

Oakes (*Old English*) From the oak trees

Oakley (*Old English*) From the field of oak trees

Obadiah (*Hebrew*) The Lord's servant

Obert (*Old German*) Wealthy leader

Octavius (*Latin*) Eighth-born child

Odell (*Old English*) One who lives in the valley

Ogden (*Old English*) From the valley with oak trees

Ogilvie (*Welsh*) High

Olaf (*Old Norse*) Ancestral heirloom

Olbracht (*Polish*) Albert

Oliver (*Latin*) Olive tree

Oliverio (*Spanish*) Oliver

Olivero (*Italian*) Oliver

Olivier (*French*) Oliver

Oman (*Scandinavian*) High protector

Omar (*Arabic*) First son/Highest

Onfroi (*French*) Humphrey

Onofre (*Spanish*) Humphrey

Onofredo (*Italian*) Humphrey

Orestes (*Greek*) Mountain man

Orion (*Greek*) Son of fire

Orman (*Old English*) Spearman

Ormond (*Old English*) Spear-protector

Oro (*Spanish*) Golden one

Orson (*Latin*) Like a bear

Orville (*Old French*) From the golden estate

Osbert (*Old English*) Divinely clever

Osborn (*Old English*) Soldier of God

Oscar *(Old Norse)* Divine spearman

Osmar *(Old English)* Divinely glorious

Osmond *(Old English)* Divine protector

Osred *(Old English)* Divine advisor

Osrig *(Old English)* Divine ruler

Oswald *(Old English)* One with divine power

Othello *(Italian)* Otto

Othniel *(Hebrew)* Lion of God

Otis *(Greek)* Keen of hearing

Otto *(Old German)* Wealthy

Owen *(Welsh)* Well-born one

P

Paavo *(Finish)* Paul

Pablo *(Spanish)* Paul

Padarn *(Welsh)* Fatherly

Paddy *See* Patrick

Padraic *(Irish)* Patrick

Padraig *(Irish)* Patrick

Padruig *(Scottish)* Patrick

Page *(French)* Young attendant

Palladin *(American Indian)* Fighter

Palmer *(Old English)* Pilgrim

Panayiotos *(Greek)* All holy

Pancras *(Greek)* All powerful

Paolo *(Italian)* Paul

Parker *(Middle English)* Guardian of the park

Parnell *(Old French)* Little Peter

Parrish *(Middle English)* From the churchyard

Pascal *(Italian)* Born at Easter

Pasquale *See* Pascal

Patrice *(French)* Patrick

Patricio *(Spanish)* Patrick

Patrick *(Latin)* Noble

Patrizio *(Italian)* Patrick

Patrizius *(German)* Patrick

Patroclus *(Greek)* His father's glory

Paul *(Latin)* Small

Paulo *(Portuguese)* Paul

Pavel *(Russian, Polish)* Paul

Pavlos *(Greek)* Paul

Paxton *(Old English)* Peace-town

Payat *(North American Indian)* He is coming

Payne *(Latin)* Villager

Paz *(Spanish)* Peace

Peadair *(Scottish)* Peter

Peadar *(Irish)* Peter

Pedr *(Welsh)* Peter

Pedro *(Spanish)* Peter

Peirce *See* Peter

Pekka *(Finnish)* Peter

Pell *(Old English)* Mantle

Pembroke *(Welsh)* Headland

Penley *(Old English)* Enclosed pasture meadow

Penn *(Latin)* Pen

Penwyn *(Welsh)* Blond

Per *(Swedish)* Peter

Percival *(Old French)* Valley piercer

Peregrine *(Latin)* Pilgrim

Pericles *(Greek)* Famous far and wide

Perry *(Middle English)* Pear tree

Perseus *(Greek)* Destroyer

Peter *(Latin)* Rock

Petros *(Greek)* Peter

Petru *(Rumanian)* Peter

Petrus *(German)* Peter

Phelan *(Irish)* Small wolf

Philaret *(Greek)* One

who loves virtue

Philip *(Greek)* One who loves horses

Philipp *(German)* Philip

Philippe *(French)* Philip

Phillip See Philip

Phineas *(Greek)* Mouth of brass

Phuong *(Vietnamese)* Fragrant

Pickford *(Old English)* From the ford at the peak

Pickworth *(Old English)* From the woodcutter's estate

Pierce *(Old French)* Rock

Pierre *(French)* Peter

Pieter *(Dutch)* Peter

Pietro *(Italian)* Peter

Piotr *(Russian)* Peter

Pirramurar *(Australian Aboriginal)* Shield

Pitney *(Old English)* Island of one who perseveres

Pitt *(Old English)* From the hollow

Plato *(Greek)* Broad-shouldered

Pollock *(Old English)* Little Paul

Pomeroy *(Old French)* From the apple orchard

Porter *(Latin)* Gatekeeper

Poul *(Danish)* Paul

Pouw *(Dutch)* Paul

Powell *(Celtic)* Son of Howell

Pradyuma *(Sanskrit)* Son of Krishna

Pramana *(Indonesian)* Wisdom

Prentice *(English)* Apprentice

Prescott *(Old English)* From the priest's home

Preston *(Old English)* Dweller at the priest's place

Price *(Old English)* Son of Rice / Ardent one

Primo *(Latin)* First-born

Probus *(Latin)* Honest

Proctor *(Latin)* Steward

Q

Quentin *(Latin)* Fifth child

Quillan *(Irish)* Cub

Quinlan *(Irish)* Strong

R

Radcliffe *(Old English)* From the red cliff

Radman *(Slavic)* Joy

Rafael *(Spanish)* Raphael

Rafaello *(Italian)* Raphael

Rafferty *(Irish)* Son of prosperity

Rafi *(Arabic)* Exalting

Raghnall *(Irish)* Ronald

Ragnar *(Norwegian)* Mighty army

Ragnor *See* Ragnar

Raimund *(German)* Raymond

Raimundo *(Spanish)* Raymond

Rainer *See* Ragnar

Rainger *See* Ranger

Rainier *(Old German)* Warrior of judgment

Raja *(Sanskrit)* Ruler

Raleigh *(Old English)* From the clearing for roe deer

Ralf *See* Ralph

Ralph *(Old English)* Fast wolf

Ralston *(Old English)* One who lives at Ralph's estate

Raman *See* Ranon

Ramiah *(Hebrew)* Praise the Lord

Ramon *(Spanish)* Raymond

Ramsay *(Old English)*

From the island of the ram

Ramsden *(Old English)* Ram's valley

Ran *(Hebrew)* Exalted

Randall *See* Randolph

Randell *See* Randolph

Randolf *See* Randolph

Randolph *(Old English)* Shield-wolf

Ranger *(Old French)* Guardian of the forest

Rankin *(Old English)* Little shield

Ranon *(Hebrew)* Joyful

Ransford *(Old English)* From the raven's ford

Ransom *(Old English)* Son of the shield

Raoul *(French)* Ralph

Raphael *(Hebrew)* God has healed

Rawiri *(Maori)* David

Rawley *See* Raleigh

Raymond *(Old English)* Powerful protector

Rayner *See* Ragnar

Reamonn *(Irish)* Raymond

Reece *(Old Welsh)* Ardent/Enthusiastic

Reed *(Old English)* Redhaired

Reg *See* Reginald

Regan *(Irish)* Little king

Reginald *(Old English)* Mighty

Reinaldo *(Spanish)* Ronald

Reinhold *(Swedish, Danish)* Ronald

Reinold *(Dutch)* Ronald

Reinwald *(German)* Ronald

Remington *(Old English)* From the raven-family estate

Remus *(Latin)* Oarsman

Renaldo *(Spanish)* Reginald

Renaud *(French)* Reynard

Renault *See* Reginald

Renè *(French)* Ronald

Renfrew *(Old Welsh)* From the placid river

Renny *(Irish)* Powerful

Renshaw *(Old English)* From the raven forest

Renton *(Old English)* Estate with roebuck deer

Reswell *See* Roswald

Reuben *(Hebrew)* Behold, a son!

Rex *(Latin)* King

Rexford *(Old English)* One who lives at the king's ford

Rey *(Spanish)* Roy

Reynard *(Old French)* Fox

Rhain *(Welsh)* Lance

Rhett *See* Rhys

Rhidian *(Welsh)* Dweller by the ford

Rhodes *(Greek)* Roses

Rhun *(Welsh)* Grand

Rhys *(Welsh)* Ardent

Ricard *See* Richard

Ricardo *(Spanish)* Richard

Riccardo *(Italian)* Richard

Richard *(Old German)* Rich and powerful ruler

Richmond *(Old German)* Powerful protector

Rick *See* Roderick

Ricky *See* Roderick

Rigby *(Old English)* Valley of the ruler

Riley *(Irish)* Valiant

Rinaldo *(Italian)* Ronald

Ringbalin *(Australian Aboriginal)* Song

Riobard *(Irish)* Robert

Riocard *(Irish)* Richard

Riordan *(Irish)* Royal bard

Roarke *(Irish)* Famous ruler

Robert *(Old English)* Shining with fame

Roberto *(Italian, Spanish)* Robert

Robin *See* Robert

Robinson *(Old English)* Son of Robin

Rochester *(Old English)* Stone fortress

Rockley *(Old English,* From the rocky meadow

Rockwell *(Old English)* From the rocky spring

Rod *See* Roderick

Roddy *See* Roderick

Roden *(Old English)* From the valley with reeds

Roderick *(Old German)* Famous ruler

Rodger *See* Roger

Rodman *(Old German)* Famous man

Rodney *(Old German)* From the clearing on the island

Rodolfo *(Italian, Spanish)* Rudolph

Rodolphe *(French)* Rudolph

Rodrick *See* Roderick

Roelof *(Dutch)* Ralph

Rogan *(Irish)* Red-haired

Roger *(Old English)* Famous spear-carrier

Rohan *See* Rowan

Roland *(Old German)* From the famous land

Rolf *(Old German)* Famous wolf

Romeo *(Italian)* Pilgrim to Rome

Ronald *(Old German)* Power

Rory *(Irish)* Red king

Roscoe *(Old Norse)* From the forest of roedeer

Roslin *(Old French)* Little red-haired one

Ross *(Irish)* Peninsula

Rosselin *See* Roslin

Rosslyn *See* Roslin

Roswald *(Old German)* Mighty with a horse

Roswell *See* Roswald

Rothwell *(Old Norse)*

From the red spring

Rover *(Old English)* Wanderer

Rowan *(Irish)* Red-haired

Rowson *(Irish)* Son of the red-haired one

Roxbury *(Old English)* From Rook's fortress

Roy *(French)* King

Royce *(Old English)* Son of the king

Ruaidhri *(Irish)* Roderick

Ruben *See* Reuben

Rudd *(Old English)* Ruddy (complexion)

Rudiger *(German)* Roger

Rudolf *(German)* Rudolph

Rudolph *(Old German)* Famous wolf

Rudyard *(Old English)* Red enclosure

Rufus *(Latin)* Red haired

Rupert *See* Robert

Ruprecht *(German)* Robert

Rupulle *(Australian Aboriginal)* Chief

Rurik *(Slavic)* Roderick

Russell *(Old English)* Foxlike

Rutherford *(Old English)* From the cattle ford

Ryan *(Irish)* Small king

Rycroft *(Old English)* From the rye field

Ryle *(Old English)* From the rye hill

Ryley *See* Riley

Ryman *(Old English)* Rye seller

S

Saber *(French)* Sword

Sacha *(Greek)* Helper

Sadaqah *(Arabic)* Truthful

Sadoc *(Hebrew)* Sacred

Safford *(Old English)* From the willow ford

Sahen *(Indian)* Falcon

Sal *See* Salvatore

Saladin *(Arabic)* Goodness of the faith

Salim *(Arabic)* Peace

Salton *(Old English)* From the manorhall town

Salvador *(Spanish)* Saviour

Salvatore *(Italian)* Salvador

Sam *See* Samuel

Sampson *(Hebrew)* Like the sun

Samson *See* Sampson

Samuel *(Hebrew)* Heard by God

Sancho *(Latin)* Sanctified

Sanders *(Middle English)* Alexander's son

Sanford *(Old English)* From the sandy ford

across the river

Sanson *(Spanish)* Sampson

Sansone *(Italian)* Sampson

Saul *(Hebrew)* One who is desired

Sauveur *(French)* Salvador

Sawyer *(Old English)* One who saws wood

Saxon *(Old English)* Swordsman

Sayed *(Arabic)* Prince

Sayer *(Celtic)* Sawyer

Scanlan *See* Scanlon

Scanlon *(Irish)* Little scandal

Schuyler *(Dutch)* Shield

Scot *(Old English)* Scotsman

Scott *See* Scot

Scotti *(Italian)* Scot

Scoville *(Old French)* From the Scotsman's village

Scully *(Irish)* Town crier

Seabert *(Old English)* Glorious as the sea

Seabright *See* Seabert

Seain *(Irish)* John

Seamus *(Irish)* Jacob

Sean *(Irish)* John

Searle *(Old German)* Warrior

Seaton *(Old French)* Sal's town

Seba *(Greek)* Majestic

Sebastian *(Latin)* Venerated

Sebastiano *(Italian)* Sebastian

Sedgley *(Old English)* From the swordsman's meadow

Sedgwick *(Old English)* Dweller at the place with sword-grass

Seeley *(Old English)* Happy

Selig *(Old German)* Blessed

Selwyn *(Old English)* Friend

Serge *(Latin)* Attendant

Sergei *(Russian)* Serge

Seth *(Hebrew)* Chosen one

Seward *(Old English)* Defender by the sea

Shai *(Hebrew)* Gift

Shakur *(Arabic)* Grateful

Shalom *(Hebrew)* Peace

Shamus *(Irish)* Jacob

Shane *(Irish)* John

Shanley *(Irish)* Old hero

Shannon *(Irish)* Wise and small

Shapoor *(Persian)* Prince

Sharif *(Arabic)* Honest

Shaun *See* John

Shaw *(Old English)* One who lives at a grove

Shawn *See* John

Shea *(Irish)* Majestic

Sheehan *(Irish)* Little peaceful one

Shelby *(Old English)*

From the ledge estate

Sheldon *(Old English)* From the ledgehill

Shelton *(Old English)* From the ledge farm

Shepley *(Old English)* From the meadow with sheep

Sherborne *(Old English)* From the clear brook

Sheridan *(Irish)* Wild savage/Satyr

Sherlock *(Old English)* Fair/Short-haired

Sherman *(Old English)* Shearer

Sidney *(Hebrew)* One who entices

Siegfried *(Old German)* Peaceful victory

Siffre *(French)* Siegfried

Sigmund *(Old German)* Victorious protector

Sigvard *(Norwegian)* Siegfried

Silas *(Latin)* Forest god

Silvester *(Latin)* From the wood

Simeon *(French)* Simon

Simon *(Hebrew)* One who hears

Simone *(Italian)* Simon

Sinclair *(Latin)* Saintly

Siomonn *(Irish)* Simon

Sion *(Hebrew)* Exalted

Skeet *(Middle English)* Swift

Skelly *(Irish)* Story-teller

Skerry *(Old Norse)* From the rocky island

Skipp *(Old Norse)* Ship owner

Slevin *(Irish)* Mountaineer

Sloan *(Irish)* Warrior

Sol *(Latin)* Sun

Solomon *(Hebrew)* Peaceful

Solomon *See* Salomon

Spencer *(Middle English)* One who dispenses provisions

Spiro *(Greek)* Breath of God

Stafford *(Old English)* Landingplace

Stan *See* Stanley

Stanford *(Old English)* Stony ford

Stanislas *(French)* Stanislaus

Stanislaus *(Slavic)* One who makes a brave stand

Stanislav *(German)* Stanislaus

Stanleigh *See* Stanley

Stanley *(Old English)* One who lives at the rocky meadow

Stanmore *(Old English)* From the rocky lake

Stanton *(Old English)* From the stony estate

Stanwick *(Old English)* Inhabitant of the rocky village

Stanwood *(Old English)* One who lives at the rocky forest

Stavropoulos *(Greek)* Son of Stavros

Stavros *(Greek)* Stephen

Steaphan *(Scottish)* Stephen

Stedman *(Old English)* Owner of a farmstead

Stefan *See* Stephen

Stefano *(Italian)* Stephen

Stein *(German)* Stone

Stepan *See* Stephen

Stephanus *(Swedish)* Stephen

Stephen *(Greek)* Crown

Sterne *(Middle English)* A stern person

Stewart *(Old English)* Steward/Bailiff

Stuart *See* Stewart

Sumner *(Middle English)* One who summons to church/Church legal officer

Sun *(Chinese)* Bending

Surya *(Sanskrit)* The sun

Susi *(Greek)* Horseman

Sutherland *(Old Norse)* From the southern land

Sutton *(Old English)* From the south estate

Sven *(Scandinavian)* Young man

Sweeney *(Irish)* Little hero

Swinton *(Old English)* Pig farmer

Sydney *See* Sidney

Sylvester *See* Silvester

Symington *(Old English)* One who lives at Simon's estate

T

Tab *(Old German)* Drummer

Tadd *(Old Welsh)* Father

Tadeo *(Spanish)* Praise

Taffy *(Welsh)* David

Taft *(Old English)* River

Taggart *(Irish)* Son of the prelate

Tait *(Scandinavian)* Great joy

Talbot *(Old English)* Bloodhound

Tangwyn *(Welsh)* Blessed peace

Tanner *(Old English)* One who tans leather

Tarleton *(Old English)* Estate of the thunder-ruler

Taro *(Japanese)* First-born son

Tarrant *(Old Welsh)* Thunder

Tavis *(Celtic)* Thomas

Tavish *(Irish)* Twin

Tayib *(Indian)* Good

Taylor *(Old English)* Tailor

Te Aroha *(Polynesian)* Man of the long string

Te-Poro *(Polynesian)* Point

Teague *(Irish)* Poet

Teangi *(Australian Aboriginal)* Earthy

Ted *See* Edward

Tellford *(Old French)* Iron ford

Templeton *(Old English)* From the town at the temple

Teobaldo *(Spanish, Italian)* Theobald

Tepko *(Australian Aboriginal)* Hill

Terence *(Latin)* Smooth/Tender

Terrell *See* Thorald

Terry *See* Terence

Thabit *(Arabic)* Firm

Thaddeus *(Latin)* One who praises

Thanh Phong *(Vietnamese)* Fresh air

Thanh *(Vietnamese)* Tranquil one

Thank Danh *(Vietnamese)* Renowned

Theobald *(Old German)* Bold chief

Theodore *(Greek)* God's gift

Theon *(Greek)* Divine

Theron *(Greek)* Hunter

Thomas *(Hebrew)* Twin

Thor *(Old Norse)* God of thunder

Thorald *(Old Norse)* Thunder-ruler

Thorbert *(Old Norse)* As glorious as thunder

Thornton *(Old English)* From the thorny town

Thorold *See* Thorald

Tiernan *(Irish)* Lord

Tim *See* Timothy

Timon *(Greek)* Honour

Timoteo *(Italian)* Timothy

Timothee *(French)* Timothy

Timotheus *(German)* Timothy

Timothy *(Greek)* Honouring God

Tiomold *(Irish)* Timothy

Titus *(Greek)* Titan/Gigantic

Tobias *(Hebrew)* God is good

Toby *See* Tobias

Todd *(Old English)* Fox

Toft *(Old English)* Small farm

Tolan *(Old English)* Owner of land subject to a toll

Tomas *(Spanish, Irish)* Thomas

Tomaso *(Italian)* Thomas

Tomkin *(Old English)* Little Tom

Tomlin *See* Tomkin

Tony *See* Anthony

Torald *See* Thorald

Torbert *See* Thorbert

Torr *(Old English)* From the tower

Townley *(Old English)* From the town meadow

Townsend *(Old English)* From the end of town

Trahern *(Old Welsh)* Great strength

Travers *(Old French)* From the crossroads

Travis *See* Travers

Tremayne *(Old Cornish)* Inhabitant of the house at the rock

Trent *(Latin)* Torrent

Trevelyan *(Old Cornish)* From Elian's homestead

Trevor *(Irish)* Wise/Prudent

Trigg *(Old Norse)* Trustworthy

Tripp *(Old English)* Traveller

Tristan *(Welsh)* Sorrowful

Tristram *See* Tristan

Troy *(Old French)* Descendant of the curly-haired people

Truman *(Old English)* Faithful man

Trung *(Vietnamese)*

Faithful

Trygve (*Scandinavian*) Protector

Tu (*Polynesian*) War/Man

Tuki (*Australian Aboriginal*) Bullfrog

Turner (*Latin*) One who works a lathe

Tut (*Arabic*) Strong/Courageous

Tybalt (*English*) Theobald

Tyler (*Old English*) One who makes tiles

Tyrell *See* Thorald

Tyrone (*Greek*) Ruler

u

Ubald (*Old German*) Mind

Uberto (*Italian*) Hubert

Udell (*Old English*) Valley of yew trees

Udolf (*Old English*) Courageous wolf

Uggieri (*Italian*) Holy

Ugo (*Italian*) Hugh

Uilleam (*Scottish*) William

Uilliam (*Irish*) William

Ulbricht *See* Albert

Ulick (*Irish*) Mind

Ulrich (*Old German*) Wolf ruler

Ulysses (*Greek*) One who hates injustice

Umberto *See* Humberto

Unwin (*Old English*) Enemy

Upton (*Old English*) Upper town

Uri (*Hebrew*) Light

Uriel (*Hebrew*) Flame of God

Uyeno (*Japanese*) Upper field

Uzi *See* Uziel

Uziel (*Hebrew*) Strength

V

Valdus (*Old German*) Power

Valentine (*Latin*) Strong/Healthy

Valentino (*Italian*) Valentine

Valerian (*Latin*) Strong

Vamana (*Sanskrit*) Deserving of praise

Vanya (*Russian*) John

Varick (*Icelandic*) Sea drifter

Vasilis (*Greek*) Knightly

Vasishtha (*Sanskrit*) Wealthy

Vaslav (*Polish*) Basil

Vassily (*Russian*) Basil

Vaughn (*Old Welsh*) Small one

Venn (*Irish*) Fair

Vern *See* Vernon

Vernon (*Latin*) Like

spring

Victor (*Latin*) Conqueror

Vilhelm (*Swedish*) William

Vincent (*Latin*) Conquering one

Vincente (*Italian, Spanish*) Vincent

Vincentius (*Dutch*) Vincent

Vincenz (*German*) Vincent

Virgil (*Latin*) Staff bearer

Vito (*Latin*) Alive

Vitorio (*Spanish*) Victor

Vittorio (*Italian*) Victor

Vladimir (*Old Slavic*) Power to rule

Vladislav (*Old Slavic*) Glorious ruler

W

Wade (*Old English*) One who advances

183

Wadsworth (*Old English*) From the advancer's estate

Wadud (*Arabic*) Loving

Wagner (*German*) Wagon-maker

Waine *See* Wayne

Wainwright (*Old English*) Wagon maker

Wajid (*Arabic*) Finder

Wakefield (*Old English*) One who lives at the wet field

Wakil (*Arabic*) Advocate

Waldemar (*Old German*) Powerful/Famous ruler

Waldo (*Old German*) Ruler

Wallace (*Old English*) Stranger

Walter (*Old German*) Powerful

Walther *See* Walter

Wang (*Chinese*) Like a king

Ward (*Old English*) Watchman

Wardell (*Old English*) From the watch-hill

Warden *See* Ward

Wardley (*Old English*) From the guardian's meadow

Warfield (*Middle English*) One who lives in the field at the weir

Warren (*Old German*) Defender

Warrick (*Old English*) Defender/Hero of the village

Warringa (*Australian Aboriginal*) The sea

Warrun (*Australian Aboriginal*) The sky

Warwick *See* Warrick

Washington (*Old English*) From the estate of the keen-one's family

Wasi (*Arabic*) Comprehensive

Wassily (*Russian*) Basil

Watford (*Old English*)

From the river crossing that is a hurdle

Wayamba *(Australian Aboriginal)* Turtle

Wayne *(Old English)* Wagon-maker

Weeronga *(Australian Aboriginal)* Quiet one

Wen Hu *(Chinese)* Educated

Wentworth *(Old English)* White one's estate

Werner *(Old German)* Defending warrior

Wernher *See* Werner

Wescott *(Old English)* One who lives at the west cottage

Wesley *(Old English)* From the west meadow

Westleigh *See* Wesley

Weston *(Old English)* From the estate in the west

Weylin *(Celtic)* Son of the wolf

Wharton *(Old English)* Estate at the hollow

Wheatley *(Old English)* Wheat meadow

Whitelaw *(Old English)* From the white hill

Whitfield *(Old English)* From the white field

Whitford *(Old English)* From the white ford

Whitley *(Old English)* From the white meadow

Whitlock *(Old English)* Man with a white lock of hair

Whitman *(Old English)* White-haired man

Whittaker *(Old English)* One who lives at the white field

Wickham *(Old English)* From the village enclosure

Wilbur *(Old German)* Resolute/Bright

Wilford *(Old English)* One who lives at the ford with willow trees

Wilfred *(Old English)* One who desires peace

Wilhelm *(German)* William

Willard *(Old German)* Resolutely brave

Willem *(Dutch)* William

William *(Old English)* Determined guardian

Willie *See* William

Wilmot *(Old German)* Resolute

Wilton *(Old English)* From the spring farm

Winfield *(Old English)* From the friend's field

Winslow *(Old English)* From the friend's hill

Winston *(Old English)* Friendly town

Winward *(Old English)* Friend's forest

Wirake *(Australian Aboriginal)* Friend

Witha *(Arabic)* Handsome

Witton *(Old English)* From the wise man's estate

Wojciech *(Slavic)* Battle soldier

Wolfe *(Old English)* Wolf

Wolfgang *(Old German)* Advancing wolf

Wollowra *(Australian Aboriginal)* Eagle

Woodrow *(Old English)* Path in the woods

Woodruff *(Old English)* Forest-warden

Wyatt *(Middle English)* Son of Guy

X, Y, Z

Xanthus *(Latin)* Golden-haired

Xavier *(Arabic)* Bright

Xenos *(Greek)* Stranger

Xerxes *(Persian)* Ruler/King

Xylon *(Greek)* From the forest

Yahbini *(Australian Aboriginal)* Star

Yahya *(Arabic)* John

Yarrawah *(Australian Aboriginal)* Storm

Yehudi *(Hebrew)* Praise God

Yestin *(Welsh)* Justin

Yevgeny *(Russian)* Eugene

Yiannis *(Greek)* John

Yin-Hsin *(Chinese)* The one force

Yorick *(Danish)* George

Yuan *(Chinese)* Original

Yul *(Mongolian)* Over the horizon

Yule *(Old English)* Born at Christmas

Yuma *(North American Indian)* Chief's son

Yung Chih *(Chinese)* Always honourable

Yung *(Chinese)* Always

Yuri *(Russian)* George

Yusseff *See* Yusuf

Yusuf *(Arabic)* Joseph

Yves *(French)* Archer

Zachariah *(Hebrew)* Jehovah's remembrance

Zachary *See* Zachariah

Zadok *(Hebrew)* Righteous one

Zane *See* John

Zbigniew *(Polish)* Denis

Zebadiah *(Hebrew)* Gift of the Lord

Zebedee *See* Zebadiah

Zeke *(Arabic)* Intelligent

Zeno *(Greek)* Stranger

Ziv *(Hebrew)* To shine

Zoltan *(Arabic)* Sultan

Zygmunt *(Polish)* Sigmund

I'm named after...

Does your baby share a birthday with a famous person? If so, you may wish to incorporate part of that name in the name you give your daughter or son. Here are some famous persons' birthdays to help you decide.

January
1 J. Edgar Hoover
2 Isaac Asimov
3 Author J.R.R. Tolkien
4 Jane Wyman
5 King Juan Carlos of Spain
6 Joan of Arc
7 "Addam's Family" creator Charles Addams
8 Elvis Presley
9 Martin Luther King
10 Rod Stewart
11 Rod Taylor
12 Joe Frazier
13 Sir Joh Bjelke-Petersen
14 Faye Dunnaway
15 Aristotle Onassis
16 Ethel Merman
17 Mohammed Ali
18 Comic actor Oliver Hardy
19 Dolly Parton
20 Slim Whitman
21 Benny Hill
22 Beatrice Potter
23 Humphrey Bogart
24 Neil Diamond
25 Robert Burns
26 Virginia Woolf
27 Wolfgang Amadeus Mozart
28 Alan Alda
29 William Claude Fields
30 Gene Hackman
31 Mario Lanza

February
1 Clark Gable
2 Farah Fawcett
3 Val Doonican
4 Alice Cooper
5 Reggae's Bob Marley
6 Ronald Reagan
7 Charles Dickens
8 James Dean
9 Mia Farrow
10 Robert Wagner
11 Thomas Edison
12 Abraham Lincoln
13 Kim Novak
14 St. Valentine
15 Jane Seymour
16 John McEnroe
17 Banjo Patterson
18 Yoko Ono Lennon
19 Lee Marvin
20 Sydney Poitier
21 Russian Czar Peter III
22 George Washington
23 George Frederick Handel
24 Alain Prost
25 Auguste Renoir
26 Victor Hugo
27 Elizabeth Taylor
28 Boxer Barry McGuigan
29 Gioacchino Rossini

March
1 David Niven
2 Singer Karen Carpenter
3 Alexander Graham Bell
4 Jean Harlow
5 Singer Elaine Page
6 Dame Kiri Te Kanawa
7 Viv Richards
8 Lynn Redgrave
9 Mickey Spillane
10 Prince Edward
11 Rupert Murdoch
12 Liza Minnelli
13 Joe Bugner

14 Albert Einstein
15 Attila the Hun
16 Matthew Flinders
17 St. Patrick
18 Nikolai
   Rimsky-Korsakov
19 Wyatt Earp
20 Dame Vera Lynn
21 Johan Sebastian
   Bach
22 Karl Malden
23 Joan Crawford
24 Steve McQueen
25 Elton John
26 Diana Ross
27 Michael York
28 Dirk Bogarde
29 Chapman Pincher
30 Rolf Harris
31 Franz Joseph Haydn

April
1 Sergei Rachmaninoff
2 Sir Jack Brabham
3 Doris Day
4 Elmar Bernstein
5 Bette Davis & Spencer
   Tracy
6 Harry Houdini
7 William Wordsworth
8 Sonja Henie
9 Hugh Heffner
10 Omar Sharif
11 Actress Jill Gascoine
12 Maria Callas
13 Thomas Jefferson
14 Rod Steiger
15 Samantha Fox

16 Spike Milligan
17 James Last
18 Albert Einstein
19 Dudley Moore
20 Ryan O'Neil
21 Queen Elizabeth
22 Alan Bond
23 William Shakespeare
24 Barbra Streisand
25 Al Pacino
26 Koo Stark
27 Samuel Morse
28 Ann-Margret
29 Emperor Hirohito
30 Pop star Bobby Vee

May
1 Glenn Ford
2 Author Jerome K.
   Jerome
3 Engelbert
   Humperdinck
4 Audrey Hepburn
5 Karl Marx
6 Robert Browning
8 Sonny Liston
9 Barbara Woodhouse
10 Pop star Donovan
11 Salvador Dali
12 Florence Nightingale
13 Joe Louis
14 Bobby Darin
15 James Mason
16 Henry Fonda
17 "Sugar" Ray
   Leonard
18 Perry Como
19 Nellie Melba

20 James Stewart
21 Fats Waller
22 Footballer George
   Best
23 Joan Collins
24 Queen Victoria
25 Marshal Tito
26 Queen Mary
27 Wild Bill Hickok
28 Patrick White
29 Bob Hope
30 Benny Goodman
31 Clint Eastwood

June
1 Superman Clark Kent
2 Johnny Weissmuller
3 Tony Curtis
4 King George III
5 Singer Bill Hayes
6 Bjorn Borg
7 Pop star Tom Jones
8 Nancy Sinatra
9 Cole Porter
10 Judy Garland
11 Jacques Yves
   Cousteau
12 Author Charles
   Kingsley
13 Poet William Butler
   Yeats
14 Burl Ives
15 Actress Nicola Pagett
16 Actor Stan Laurel
17 Barry Manilow
18 Garfield
19 Duchess of Windsor
   Bessie Wallis Warfield

20 Errol Flynn
21 Jean-Paul Sartre
22 Meryl Streep
23 Sir Leonard Hutton
24 Horatio Herbert, Lord Kitchener
25 George Orwell
26 Colonel Tom Parker
27 France's King Louis XII
28 Mel Brooks
29 Nelson Eddy
30 Mike Tyson

July

1 Princess Diana
2 Norway's King Olaf V
3 Richard Hadlee
4 Gina Lollobrigida
5 Phineas Taylor Barnum
6 Sylvester Stallone
7 Ringo Starr
8 John Davison Rockefeller
9 Barbara Cartland
10 Marcel Proust
11 Yul Brynner
12 Henry Thoreau
13 Harrison Ford
14 Ingmar Bergman
15 Linda Rondstadt
16 Roald Amundsen
17 Donald Sutherland
18 John Glenn
19 Ile Nastase
20 Sir Edmund Hillary
21 Swazi King Sobhuza the Second
22 Terence Stamp
23 Emperor Haile Selassie
24 Amelia Earhart
25 First test-tube baby Louise Brown
26 Mick Jagger
27 Allan Border
28 Sir Garfield Sober
29 Benito Mussolini
30 Henry Ford
31 Evonne Goolagong

August

1 Yves St Laurent
2 Peter O'Toole
3 Martin Sheen
4 Percy Bysshe Shelley
5 Harold Holt
6 Robert Mitchum
7 Greg Chappell
8 Dustin Hoffman
9 Rod Laver
10 Herbert Hoover
11 Alex Haley
12 Cecil Blount De Mille
13 Alfred Hitchcock
14 Sarah Brightman
15 Napoleon Bonaparte
16 Madonna
17 Mae West
18 Robert Redford
19 Orville Wright
20 John Emburey
21 Princess Margaret
22 Claude Debussy
23 Golfer Peter Thomson
24 Max Beerbohm
25 Elvis Costello
26 John Buchan
27 Tarzan of the Apes
28 Goethe
29 Michael Jackson
30 Frankenstein creator Mary Shelley
31 James Coburn

September

1 Engelbert Humperdick
2 Russ Conway
3 Alan Ladd
4 Dawn Fraser
5 Racquel Welch
6 Jackie Trent
7 John McDouall Stuart
8 Peter Sellers
9 Cardinal Richelieu
10 Arnold Palmer
11 Ferdinand Marcos
12 Maurice Chevalier
13 Claudette Colbert
14 Actor Jack Hawkins
15 Agatha Christie
16 Peter Falk
17 Roddy McDowell
18 Mahatma Gandhi
19 Mickey Mouse
20 Sofia Loren
21 H.G. Wells
22 Captain Mark Phillips
23 Bruce Springsteen
24 Linda McCartney
25 Ronnie Barker

'I was named after...'

26 Ian Chappell
27 Pop star Alvin
   Stardust
28 Brigitte Bardot
29 Jerry Lee Lewis
30 Deborah Kerr

October
1 Walter Matthau
2 Groucho Marx
3 Chubby Checker
4 Charlton Heston
5 Bob Geldof
6 Tony Greig
7 Clive James
8 Juan Peron
9 John Lennon
10 James Clavell
11 Bobby Charlton
12 Luciano Pavarotti
13 Margaret Thatcher
14 Cliff Richard
15 John L. Sullivan
16 Oscar Wilde
17 Evel Knievel
18 Chuck Berry
19 Adam Lindsay
   Gordon
20 Bela Lugosi
21 Alfred Nobel
22 Joan Fontaine
23 Diana Dors
24 The Big Bopper
25 Helen Reddy
26 Mahalia Jackson
27 John Cleese
28 Hank Marvin

29 Joseph Goebbels
30 Henry "The Fonz"
   Winkler
31 Eddie Charlton

November
1 Gary Player
2 Marie Antoinette
3 Charles Bronson
4 Loretta Swit
5 Lester Piggott
6 Ray Coniff
7 Marie Curie
8 Alain Delon
9 Hedy Lamarr
10 Richard Burton
11 Rodney Marsh
12 Grace Kelly
13 Robert Louis
   Stevenson
14 Prince Charles
15 Mantovani
16 Frank Bruno
17 Sir Charles
   Mackerras
18 George Gallup
19 Jodie Foster
20 Robert Kennedy
21 Goldie Hawn
22 Tom Conti
23 Billy the Kid
   (William Bonney)
24 Ian Botham
25 Karl Friedrich Benz
26 Tina Turner
27 Jimi Hendrix
28 Randy Newman

29 Louise May Alcott
30 Winston Churchill

December
1 Madame Tussaud
2 Painter George Seurat
3 Joseph Conrad
4 Pamela Stephenson
5 Walt Disney
6 Ira Gershwin
7 Eli Wallach
8 Sammy Davis Jr
9 Kirk Douglas
10 Jahangir Khan
11 Singer Brenda Lee
12 Frank Sinatra
13 Dick van Dyke
14 Nostradamus
15 John Paul Getty
16 Noel Coward
17 Kerry Packer
18 Betty Grable
19 Edith Piaf
20 Sir Robert Menzies
21 Frank Zappa
22 Dame Peggy Ashcroft
23 J(oseph) Arthur
   Rank
24 Colin Cowdrey
25 Sissy Spacek
26 Richard Widmark
27 Marlene Dietrich
28 Maggie Smith
29 Mary Tyler Moore
30 Rudyard Kipling
31 John Denver

YOUR BABY'S EXCLUSIVE PERSONAL HOROSCOPE

Here's your chance to receive a *FREE* personal horoscope prepared exclusively for your baby by the famous astrologer Madame Carmen Zofirski. The 10-page natal horoscope comes to you printed on de-luxe heavy paper in the name of your baby, creating a perfect companion for your copy of *Australian Baby Names and Memories* and a lifelong keepsake.

To make the natal horoscope completely accurate, complete the form below with your baby's FULL NAMES, the TOWN and STATE where your baby was born, as well as the exact TIME AND DATE OF THE BIRTH. However, if you do not have the exact time, you can simply indicate "A.M." or "P.M."

The natal horoscope, which will be calculated specially for your baby using the most modern and accurate techniques known to astrologers, examines in detail the influence on his or her life of each of the eight planets, as well as of the sun and moon. Because it is compiled from personal information about your child, this natal horoscope is far more accurate than general horoscopes which look merely at the broad categories of star signs.

To receive your baby's personal horoscope, simply complete the form below and mail it, together with postage stamps to the value of $4.60 to cover postage and handling, to: Carmen Zofirski, c/o Publishing Management Pty Ltd, PO Box 529, Kiama, NSW 2533.

BABY NAMES & MEMORIES PERSONAL HOROSCOPE OFFER

Enclosed please find postage stamps to the value of $4.60 to cover postage and handling charges. Please rush me a personal horoscope for my Daughter/Son:

First names: _____

Family name: _____

Date of birth: _____ Time of birth: _____ A.M./P.M.

Town of birth: _____ State: _____

Please send the horoscope within 14-days to:

Name: _____

Street: _____

Town: _____ P/Code: _____

Mail to: Carmen Zofirski, Publishing Management Pty Ltd, PO Box 529, Kiama, NSW 2533.